The 100 Most Pointless Arguments in the
World . . . Solved

# The 100 Most Pointless Arguments in the World . . . Solved

## Alexander Armstrong and Richard Osman

CORONET

First published in Great Britain in 2013 by Coronet
An imprint of Hodder & Stoughton
An Hachette UK company

First published in paperback in 2014

2

A CIP catalogue record for this title is available from the British Library

ISBN 978 1 444 76208 2

Typeset in Celeste 11/16 pt by
Palimpsest Book Production Limited, Falkirk, Stirlingshire
Printed and bound by Clays Ltd, St Ives plc

Hodder & Stoughton policy is to use papers that are natural,
renewable and recyclable products and made from wood grown
in sustainable forests. The logging and manufacturing processes
are expected to conform to the environmental regulations of the
country of origin.

Hodder & Stoughton Ltd
338 Euston Road
London NW1 3BH

www.hodder.co.uk

To my amazing Mum, Brenda Osman,
who taught me how to argue in the first place.

To my parents, Angus and Virginia Armstrong,
with apologies for the many pointless arguments
I have waged over the years.

# ACKNOWLEDGEMENTS

We would like to take a moment to thank the following people for their enormous help in writing this book. Maybe three moments. You could time us if you like?

Thanks to the all-important Pointless producers, David Flynn, Michelle Woods, James Fox and Tara Ali. We have listed them in order of their 'importance'. If you want them ranked in order of who does the actual work, simply read the list backwards.

The ever brilliant Pointless question team. Smart, funny, buff (have you guys been working out?) and a genuinely terrific pub quiz team. Bronagh Taggart, Simon Magson, Rose 'Awesome' Dawson, Tom Garton, Laura Ellis, Rob Watts, Helen Morris, Big Nick Shearing (he's not really big, he's normal-sized, but that wouldn't work as a nickname), Jennifer Blyth and Oliver Duffin.

Special thanks to Chris 'Halestorm' Hale, for his usual brilliance, and to Stewart McCartney for his unusual brilliance.

Talking of brilliance, our thanks to the wonderful Debbie Dannell, Pauline Simmons, Lisa Mejuto, Gill Smith, Frosty, Paul 'Floor Paulie' Morgan and Sharon Smith. None of you must ever tell the world what we are really like.

For suggesting 'Pointless' arguments we are indebted to some lovely 'Pointless' viewers, Mark Rea, Lucy Lappin, Katherine Rigby, Steve Murray, Gina Loizou, Rachel Adamantos, Sam Mould and Blair MacDonald. Thanks to everybody else who sent in suggestions too.

Thanks also to all the grown-ups, Fiona Rose and Mark Booth at Hodder & Stoughton, Lucas Church and Claire Heys at Endemol and the wonderful Pam Cavannagh at the BBC. And we missed Charlotte Hardman this time, so instead, a big hello to Alfie Hardman.

Penultimately, but not penultimateleastly thanks to the very funny and handsome Colin Swash, Aidan Hawkes and Matt Hulme.

But biggest thanks of all from us both, to our 'Pointless' Series Producer, John Ryan. He makes the show so much easier and our jobs so much more fun. No argument.

# CONTENTS

# 100
# INTRODUCTION

How much time do you *waste* having arguments? (Does God exist? Does your husband *really* have man-flu? Which one is Ant?) An hour a day? Two hours a day? You are probably now arguing with somebody about how long you spend arguing every day. So, in this book we're going to take the 100 most pointless arguments of all time, and we're going to solve *every single one of them*, once and for all. Are ghosts real? Which way around should the toilet roll hang? You're about to find out.

Here's the basic idea. Next time any pointless argument crops up at home, at work, at school or, more unusually, in a hot-air balloon, simply take out this book, turn to the relevant chapter, point to the definitive answer and move on. Think of the time you'll save. Either one or two hours a day.

You'll also find lots of fiendish play-along *Pointless* quizzes to annoy all the family.

In fact I think it's safe to say that . . .

 Hi, Richard!

 Oh. Xander, hi. You're back early.

 Squash was cancelled – John's pulled his hamstring. What are you doing?

 Me? Nothing. Just some admin.

 It's just that it looks like you might be writing the introduction to our new book?

 I'm not! I'm . . . Well, yes, I'm making notes about the introduction.

 I thought you said I could write it this year?

 You know when the deadline is, yes?

 No – soonish?

 Four weeks ago.

 Ah . . . That's why we're getting all those emails?

 Yes.

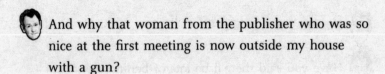 And why that woman from the publisher who was so nice at the first meeting is now outside my house with a gun?

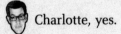 Charlotte, yes.

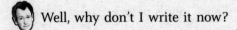 Well, why don't I write it now?

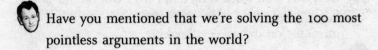 Oh, man, that would be a great idea. But I've sort of done it already is the thing.

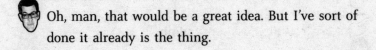 Have you mentioned that we're solving the 100 most pointless arguments in the world?

 Yep.

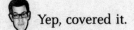 And that there will be lots of quizzes from the show for people to play against their families?

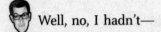 Yep, covered it.

And that we're solving lots of viewers' arguments too?

Well, no, I hadn't—

Ooh, and have you said how much we love making the show, and writing the book?

No, but I was going—

 Have you said there'll be lots of behind-the-scenes gossip about the show?

 Not yet, but—

 Like that time you smuggled those two Guatamalan w—

 Hey, here's an idea! Why don't we write the introduction together?

 Perfect!

 Shall we begin?

 Well, we've sort of done it, haven't we?

 I suppose so. We could say thank you to everyone for watching.

 Ooh, yes, that's good. Say that.

 Anything else you want to add?

 I would like to add that I have lost my keys.

OK. That doesn't need to be in the introduction, though, does it?

 No, you're quite right.

 So shall we just solve another ninety-nine arguments?

 I think we should. Before Charlotte reloads.

# WHOSE TURN IS IT TO TAKE THE BINS OUT?

This is the perfect place to start the book, as 'Whose turn is it to take the bins out?' opens the single most common argument in Britain today.*

At first it seems like a perfectly innocent query, but we all know better than that, don't we?

When the words 'Whose turn is it to take the bins out?' enter any conversation, your brain instantly issues an 'Amber Level Alert', which, as we all know, signifies 'Deadly Threat Imminent'.

When you hear 'Whose turn is it to take the bins out?' from

.........................................................................

* A closely related argument is 'Whose turn is it to chase after the bin lorry because you hadn't realised today was bin day until you heard the lorry trundling by, thanks to forgetting there was a bank holiday?'

your wife, you know the question you're actually hearing is: 'Remind me again why I married you?' And who, quite honestly, still has a convincing answer to that one?

When you hear 'Whose turn is it to take the bins out?' from your husband, however, you know the question you're actually hearing is slightly more complicated. What you are hearing is this:

'Look, we both know I keep a colour-coded chart outlining whose turn it is to take the bins out. I admit I do this largely because this is the only household task I regularly share with you. Though I do sometimes do the drying up, remember? But that aside, the fact I'm raising it can mean only one thing. I know for a fact that it's your turn and for once I've decided to make an issue of it. Why am I making it an issue today? Who knows? Let's assume my male ego has been damaged in some way. Maybe I can't actually fit into those trousers you told me to try on before I bought them, but which I didn't bother to. Either way, I am now questioning my very role as a man, and resenting the stereotypes that have forced me to live my life as a bumbling male cliché, which, on this particular occasion, is being played out in the form of you expecting me, actually quite reasonably, to put the bins out. But is this all I am? This hopeless but dependable fool? That is what my life has come to? I could have been a spy, or a motorbike stunt rider. Probably still could if I put my mind to it. I'm only in my forties, for goodness' sake. That's it! That's it! Tomorrow I'm going to start going to the gym again. I bet I could do a triathlon this summer. That'll show everyone. Now, wait, hold on, what was I talking about again?'

I'm going to assume that nobody wants to have either of the discussions above. Wouldn't it be simpler just to take the bins out yourself, then settle in for an evening of watching *The Great British Bake Off*? Maybe Dave could even show you those trousers he bought earlier.

Therefore, the answer to the argument 'Whose turn is it to take the bins out?' should always be . . .

I THINK IT'S MY TURN.

# 98

# SHOULD WE DO A NUDE CALENDAR THIS YEAR?

It's a big question. The sort of question that has Harvard Business School graduates earnestly scratching their heads and groins. Would Woolworths still be a going concern if their board of directors had done a nude calendar? If Lehman Brothers had only taken the care to produce twelve tastefully lit tableaux of unclothed senior partners in a combination of wry and witty scenarios, might the crash have been averted? These, as I say, are questions for academics of a subsequent generation. What you want to know is, 'Should *you* do a nude calendar?'

Assuming you're a small business or charity (and not, say, a care home or a backbench committee) and you've got at least twelve people willing to model, then there's a strong argument that says, 'Yes, you should.'* It's not going to cost you

.......................................................................................

* Obviously if it's just going to be one person featuring throughout

very much to put together (Dave the printer told Yvonne at the Christmas party that he would do her a nude calendar for *nothing*). And there you go: you've got twelve families geared up to buy at least one calendar each. Again, it should ideally be done to raise money rather than simply 'awareness' because – in any sense of the phrase – no one's buying that.

The trick with this, though, is to be original, and this is where the arguments begin to stack up against you (much like the cream buns did against Celia Imrie in 'November') because this is an idea that has been done a couple of times before. Below I outline some original directions to consider.

## JANUARY

Colin from HR running nude across the pitch at Murrayfield surrounded by five members of the Lothian & Borders Police. Were it not for a carefully placed police helmet Col would be demonstrating *his* devastating tackle.**

## MARCH

Karen and Lorraine from Reception and Becki who used to
..........................
then it looks less 'everyone in it for a lark' and more 'someone seriously needs to have a word with Sandra'.
** Mind you, Sergeant McLintock has no right there to be attempting an Up and Under.

work in Simon Anderson's office caught on CCTV at 1.56 a.m. on Saturday, 2 March 2013, having a wee at the cashpoint next to the Lakeland in Market Street.

## JUNE

James from Development and an unidentified brunette photographed nude in club class on a flight to Houston. Mid-flight is no time for the undercarriage to come out! Only a few strategically placed horrified onlookers and cabin crew protecting their modesty!***

## SEPTEMBER

A nude of Tahir from PR and Marketing handcuffed to a lamppost outside O'Donoghue's bar in Dublin. Is that a lamppost, Taz? Or are you just . . . Actually, yes, it is a lamppost. And, no, you're not pleased to see me, not with a camera. No, not at all.

## NOVEMBER

Trudi from Recruitment and her husband tastefully shot through the window of their VW Passat TDI at the Forest Burn layby. Eagle-eyed calendar buyers will also see the

...............................................................................

*** Amid all the turbulence they should, if nothing else, be wearing their seatbelts.

reflection of Jason Macgillivray, our CEO – not such a bored member on this occasion, Jason!

Should you do a nude calendar this year? Of course you should. Will it make money? It doesn't matter. Even if it's a heinous embarrassment to one and all, your 'Not Really Nude' nude calendar will be a salutary experience, and who knows? Maybe it will speed the day when this terrible craze for plagiaristic exhibitionism is a thing of the distant past.

# 97
# CATS V. DOGS

Why am I doing this? What an absolute fool I am. Why even *include* 'Cats v. Dogs' in the book? Whichever conclusion I reach, so many people are going to be furious with me. And I *hate* people being furious with me. I like it when people say, 'I'll tell you who's a helluva guy. Richard from *Pointless*,' or 'I bumped into Richard from *Pointless* the other day, and he *could not* have been nicer. Handshake like an ox too.'

But here we are, and I have to make a very tough decision, one that will . . . Wait a minute, I have an idea! A *terrific* idea! Where's my mobile? Ah, yes, in my hand as always.

 Hello.

 Xander! How are you?

 You see me every day, you know how I am.

Hahaha! Classic Xander. Anyway, some bad news I'm afraid. I've broken both my hands.

 You're not serious?

 Afraid so. I was putting the bins out – even though I'm not absolutely certain it was my turn – and I had a severe lid accident.

 Oh, God, is there anything I can do?

 That's very thoughtful. Could you possibly write the 'Cats v. Dogs' section of the book for me?

 Hahahahahahahahahaha! Nice try, Osman!

 No, I'm serious, I just—

 Hahahahaha! I'm just going into a tunnel. See you tomorrow!

Going into a tunnel? On his landline? Hmm. OK, still me, then. Let's get this over with.

Cats and dogs are both lovely. I adore them with every ounce of my being. But I have to choose just one – you understand that, don't you? You recognise the position I'm in?

Here's the way I'm going to approach this. I want you to think about your closest friends. I would argue that there are three things you value in them above all else:

1. They are loyal.
2. They make you laugh.
3. They are slightly more stupid than you.

You have just, of course, described a dog.

Now take a look at your other friends. I'm sure we all have one who fits the following description:

1. They only call when they need something.
2. They only like the most expensive food you can possibly provide them with.
3. Every now and again, for no explicable reason, you wake up with their backside in your face.

Yes, you've just described a cat.

Of course we love this second friend too. This is our 'cool' friend, who stays up all night, doing who knows what, and doing who knows who. The friend with no money who is always so perfectly groomed. The friend who, just as you reach the end of your tether and decide they're more trouble than they're worth, will do something so unutterably lovely and charming that you instantly remember why you love them so much.

I suppose, in summary, if cats and dogs *were* people, you would sleep with a cat, but marry a dog.

(Incidentally, there is a special prize to anyone who can point out all seventeen awful things wrong with that sentence.)

So, by now you know where I'm going. There are cat lovers, there are dog lovers, and there are lovers of both. I'm both. You can keep your rabbits, your hamsters and your goldfish; cats and dogs are head, shoulders and paws above them all. But who wins 'Cats v. Dogs'?

Dogs.

## POINTLESS FACTS

People with cats are more likely to have university degrees than those with dogs, according to a scientific survey of pet ownership.

Some famous people apparently had ailrophobia – a fear of cats: Alexander the Great, Julius Caesar, Genghis Khan, Ivan the Terrible, William Shakespeare, Louis XIV, Napoleon Bonaparte, Isadora Duncan, Benito Mussolini and Adolf Hitler. Oh, and Dwight D. Eisenhower had his staff shoot any cats seen on the grounds of his home.

# 96

## WHO WAS THE BEST BOND?

We might as well do this one, mightn't we, seeing as we're here, gathered around one of the stickier tables in literature's first ever virtual pub? Richard's just gone to the bar to get a round in (72,414 pints of lager, 12,275 glasses of dry white wine, 4,008 pints of Guinness and one WKD).* So we could use this moment to discuss who our favourite Bond actor is, and when Richard gets back with the drinks in about sixty-five days' time,** we can surprise him by having worked something out for ourselves. He'll really like that.

Everyone has a strong view on their favourite Bond actor, and although it's usually held with the tenacity of a man clinging to the top of the Eiffel Tower or the bottom of a

......................................................................

* For himself.
** Irritatingly, literature's first ever virtual pub has only got one lager on tap.

helicopter, I think we can probably reduce our field here without upsetting too many people. There are, let's be honest, two favourites. And I mean that as no criticism of any of you, George, Timmy, Pierce or Daniel,\*\*\* it's just that the Connery and Moore Bonds each spanned huge chunks of people's lives (Connery, nine years and six official films;\*\*\*\* Moore, twelve years and seven films). It's not out of the question that in fifteen years' time Daniel Craig will have broodingly shot and shagged his way to the top and eclipsed the Connery/Moore incumbencies but for now it's Monnery (SeRo?) that rules the roost.\*\*\*\*\*

But how do we even begin to separate the two most famous hands to have fired a shot from a Walther PPK, cupped so many exotic breasts, found so many enterprising ways of dispatching scary big sidekicks, and to have turned so many expensive steering-wheels at speed? Connery was the taller Bond (six foot three to Moore's six foot one) but Moore was the lighter-hearted. Mind you, each of these features can work

..................................................................................

\*\*\* They're also in our pub. Say hello, everyone. So, George, what have you been up to?

\*\*\*\* The unofficial one is, of course, *Never Say Never Again* – advice that perhaps Sean should have ignored.

\*\*\*\*\* I have long enjoyed lobbing the Dalton bomb into this discussion – I genuinely think that he is the best *actor* to play Bond. Not necessarily the best Bond, his turn in *The Living Daylights* displayed a different level of acting skills from anything seen before.

both ways. Tall and light-hearted may be more attractive, but if your job is spying, excessive height will only draw attention.

Connery was the original Bond, but for anyone who grew up in the seventies,****** Moore was the first Bond we saw in action. Connery carried off a tuxedo (and cigarette) with aplomb while Roger Moore made the safari suit (briefly) an object of unimaginable desirability – matching jacket and shorts, what's not to like? Connery was dark and brooding, Moore urbane and fair . . .

Oh, this is no good. We're not getting anywhere and nearly ten thousand people have drifted over to the *Deal or No Deal* machine in the corner. We need an answer. So, here goes.

Everyone's favourite Bond is initially the first actor they knew in the part. Then they get a bit older, live through more dull family Christmases and get to know all the films, and they rethink.

OK, if you hold a gun to my head. Or strap me to a table with a laser pointed at my genitals . . .

The best Bond? It's Connery. Sean Connery.

..................................................................................

****** Not that anyone really *grew up* in the seventies. We all just got a bit older.

Ah, Richard, perfect timing! Wow, what a big tray. Cheers!

Hang on, you forgot the crisps.

## POINTLESS FACTS

Ian Fleming offered the role of Dr No to Noël Coward, who replied by telegram: 'Dr No? No! No!!'

A boy called Scaramanga and Ian Fleming apparently had a number of playground fights at Eton.

Explorer Sir Ranulph Fiennes auditioned to become James Bond, after Sean Connery. He was in the last six and had a meeting with producer Cubby Broccoli, but Broccoli said that his hands were too big and he had the face of a farmer. Roger Moore got the part.

Sean Connery started losing his hair at twenty-one. He wore a toupee in his James Bond films.

# 95

# DO I HAVE THE WORST CATCHPHRASE IN THE WORLD?

I have a number of catchphrases on *Pointless*. For example:

'Hiya, hello.'

'Well done if you got that at home.'

'I'll give you the correct answer at the end of the pass.'

'Sorry, Gordon, Midge Ure was not a pre-war British prime minister.'

Xander, of course, has . . .

'Would the second players please take their places at the podium.'

'Very good indeed.'

'My drinking is *not* an issue. If I want to record a
show drunk it is *my* business, not yours, not the
BBC's, *mine*. Now, somebody help me off the floor.
And I'm going to need new trousers.'

But the catchphrase that I think sums up the maverick, devil-
may-care attitude of *Pointless* more than any other is . . .

'And by "country" we mean a sovereign state that is a
member of the UN in its own right.'

Just out of interest for *Pointless* trivia fans (which, by definition, is sort of all of you), for the first two hundred shows
or so, I used to say, 'And by "country" we mean a member
of the UN that is a sovereign state in its own right', until one
day I took a proper look at it and realised I'd been saying it
wrong. And I'm not even the one who drinks heavily.

Below are thirteen famous game-show catchphrases and mine
is definitively worse than every single one of them.

So, do I have the worst catchphrase in game-show history?
I'll give you the correct answer at the end of the pass.*

Which famous game shows are the following catchphrases
from?

...........................................................................................

* Yes, I do.

# POINTLESS QUIZ

1. 'You get nothing for a pair . . .'
2. 'Can I have a "P" please, Bob?'
3. 'Come on down!'
4. 'Let's go channel-hopping'
5. 'Your chosen specialised subject'
6. 'A question for father and eldest child only'
7. 'Our survey said . . .'
8. 'Who lives in a house like this?'
9. 'Your starter for ten'
10. 'Question or nominate?'
11. 'Let's go to the destination board'
12. 'Phone a friend'
13. 'Uvavu'

# 94

## SHOULD I GO UP THE A19, ROUND THE A407, AND ONTO THE A1? OR SHOULD I WIGGLE MY WAY DIRECT ON ALL THE LITTLE ROADS?

You should go up the A19, around the A407, and onto the A1. Much quicker.

# 93

# ARE GHOSTS REAL?

This seems a reasonable argument to have, given that so many people have reported seeing ghosts. Occasionally someone sane and rational, whom you wouldn't automatically avoid at a party, sees a ghost. So, is there something in it? Let's find out.

Scientists like to explain away ghostly encounters. They cite such things as 'evidence' and 'experiments' and 'the fact that most people who see a ghost are either asleep, drunk or American'. But surely there are many things in the world that simply *cannot* be explained, Jedward being one example. Or possibly two examples.

And also scientists don't have *all* the answers, do they? If scientists knew everything, then why would they continue to have that same haircut? And would buying some nice shoes kill them?

But despite all of this I don't believe in ghosts. And here's why. As with so many of the great things in life, it involves some simple maths. Ghost maths!

Let's start by assuming that people who say they've seen a ghost actually *have* seen a ghost. They have had a genuine encounter with the soul of a dead person. If we take their experiences as a starting point we can conclude the following things, all of which seem fairly universal to ghost sightings:

**GHOSTS CAN BE VISIBLE.**

**GHOSTS ARE ABLE TO COMMUNICATE WITH US AND OFTEN HAVE SPECIFIC MESSAGES TO REPORT.**

**MOST GHOSTS SEEM TO HAVE NO PHYSICAL BARRIERS.**

Now let's do that tiny bit of maths. Since the beginning of time, nearly six billion human beings have died. Let's assume that not everyone can become a ghost (that would be *crazy*), but assume instead that perhaps one in 100 people will become a ghost (by and large they will be famous people or spurned women in long dresses).

That gives us sixty million ghosts. *Sixty million!* And given that ghosts don't die, let's assume they're capable of hanging around for a while. So we have sixty million ghosts, equivalent to the entire population of the UK, *all* capable of being visible, *all* capable of moving anywhere at will, and many with a desire to communicate something specific.

What would the world be like if we accept that these things are true? We wouldn't be able to *move* for ghosts.

And yet *not a single one* of these sixty million ghosts has ever thought of proving their existence once and for all by – just as a simple example – turning up unannounced on *The One Show*. Honestly, what's to stop them? It's on every day! Most of you ghosts can feel free to carry on appearing late at night in a dusty corner of an old house, in front of a sleepy child. We only need *one of you* to breeze in next to Matt Baker and Alex Jones at about ten past seven any weekday evening. Settle back, tell us who you are and the message you have to impart. Tell Dave you forgive him, or let Sue know where you left the savings book. You could even meet Phil Tufnell if he's on. Come on, ghosts!

Apart from anything it would be a ratings bonanza and I can almost guarantee you'd get a regular slot on the show: 'Joining us later on *The One Show*, Ainsley Harriott will be showing us the secrets of Caribbean cookery, Gyles Brandreth is at the Keswick Pencil Museum, and Eddie the ghost will be telling us what JFK makes of the new One Direction single.'

There are many good things about believing that our spirits live on after our deaths. The spirits of those people we loved and who loved us, of course, do live on in our hearts and our memories.

But the fact that not one ghost has ever appeared on *The One Show* is conclusive proof that ghosts don't exist.

## POINTLESS FACT

Anne Boleyn not only haunts the Tower of London, but the church of St Peter ad Vincula (St Peter in Chains), also in London, Hever Castle in Kent and Blickling Hall, Norfolk. She has yet to be on *The One Show*.

# 92

## AM I TOO OLD TO WEAR THIS?

INT. BUSY GASTRO-PUB EARLY EVENING

ED, SARAH, VICKY AND SAUL ARE STANDING AT THE
BAR OF THE HAUNCH OF VENISON, A RURAL PUB THAT
IS FILLING UP WITH A FRIDAY NIGHT CROWD.

**ED**

I'm amazed you got a table here. We tried last summer
and they said not a chance, booked for months. How'd
you do it?

**VICKY**

Oh, Saul does their accounts so . . .

**SARAH**

See, Edward, you need to start using your clout.

**ED**

I don't think estate agents get any clout. We get a free
Mini instead. So, are Danny and Mia coming?

**SAUL**

Think so. They were having problems getting a babysitter but we haven't heard anything so I presume they're still on.

**VICKY**

No news is good news. Aha, talk of the devil!

AT THAT MOMENT DANNY AND MIA WALK IN. THE PUB QUIETENS. MIA IS NORMALLY DRESSED BUT DANNY IS WEARING A ONESIE WITH GRAFFITI WRITING ALL OVER IT.

**SAUL**

Mia (*kiss*), Danny (*manly handshake*), how are you? We've just got some drinks – what'll you have?

**ED**

Wow, Danny, you're looking, erm, looking very . . . What have you done? Something's different.

**DANNY**

Beer for me, thanks, Saul. I dunno . . . Erm, haircut? Had a trim last week.

**ED**

Maybe. Darling, why's Danny looking so amazing? You've lost weight or something.

**SARAH**

No! Typical man – doesn't notice anything. It's the onesie. Danny, my God, you look incredible. Where did you get it?

**DANNY**

Oh, this? Urban Outfitters.

**VICKY**

It's unbelievable. (*Touching her neck*) Shit, Danny, I can hardly believe it's you. I actually want to take you outside to the car-park and have noisy sex with you.

**ED**

Do you want the keys to the Mini?

**SAUL**

Uh, steady on, Vicks . . .

**VICKY**

Sorry, Saul, love, but look at him.

**SARAH**

She's right. Sweet Jesus, Danny, you're actually making me hot and prickly. Take me right here, Danny boy, right in this bar. I don't care who sees.


AS SARAH SITS UP ON THE BAR THE MAÎTRE D' APPROACHES DANNY.

HE IS OPENING A BOTTLE OF CHAMPAGNE.

**MAÎTRE D'**

Excuse me, sir, the manager has asked me to send this over for the sexy man in the onesie. I hope that meets with your approval.


VICKY HAS RIPPED OPEN HER BLOUSE AND SARAH IS NOW LYING DOWN ON THE BAR, MEWING LIKE A CAT. DANNY STARTS TO UNDO HIS ONESIE.

**SARAH**

No!

**VICKY**

No! Leave the onesie on.

**SARAH**

Leave it on!

**VICKY**

I want to SEE IT! I HAVE TO SEE THE ONESIE—

**AND . . . WAKE UP.**

Put the onesie back on its hanger and walk out of the shop.

Are you too old to wear that? Yes, of course you are.

# 91

## WHO WOULD WIN IN A FIGHT BETWEEN...?

Alcohol is responsible for many things. Laughs, tears and, if you're being honest, your second child. But it is also responsible for over 40 million 'Who would win in a fight between ...?' conversations. Let's settle each and every one of them once and for all.

### LION V. TIGER

The lion and tiger would only meet on a ferry somewhere between Asia and Africa. Or perhaps in a zoo with very, very lax security. Both animals are of broadly equivalent size, but the lion is much more used to hunting in packs, and to toying with its prey, whereas a tiger hunts alone and always goes for the kill. Given that, I have to hand this fight to . . .

THE TIGER

### MUHAMMAD ALI V. MIKE TYSON

If each were at his peak who would win? The awesome

brutality of Tyson, or the immense athleticism and intelligence of Ali?

Ali is too cute to be caught out by an early Tyson onslaught, and as Tyson tires Ali starts to dominate. Tough for either to knock the other out, so this one, unlike lion v. tiger, goes to the judges' scorecards. Those judges are me and two of my friends who were in the pub this evening. And we scored it for . . .

MUHAMMAD ALI

### DARTH VADER V. JAMES BOND

Darth Vader was (spoiler alert) killed by Emperor Palpatine, and even had his hand cut off by his own son. No one has ever killed James Bond, and he rarely even loses a cufflink.

Darth Vader is not essential to the *Star Wars* franchise, but James Bond is pretty central to the James Bond franchise, so Hollywood money-men would never allow Bond to die. And so . . .

JAMES BOND

### YOUR MUM V. MY MUM

No contest . . .

MY MUM

OK, that's all settled. Let's have some more alcohol. What shall we talk about now? We've done all the who'd-win-a-fight conversations, haven't we? The tiger won, and Ali, then James Bond and my mum. Hold on! That gives me an idea! Semi-finals!

### TIGER V. MUHAMMAD ALI

Ali can 'bob and weave' and 'rope-a-dope' all he likes, but a tiger can leap horizontally into the air, baring razor-sharp teeth in a way that George Foreman never quite managed. This probably wouldn't go to the judges' scorecards. In fact, the judges would also be mauled to death. I really can't believe we didn't put more thought into the organisation of this fight. Winner . . .

THE TIGER

### JAMES BOND V. MY MUM

I'm as big a fan of my mum as you're likely to find, but even I have to concede this one to . . .

JAMES BOND

This is now getting very exciting. If a bit messy. And for everyone who is worried, my mum is OK, just concussion and bruising. And she was very excited to meet Daniel Craig.

And now we're super-drunk it's time for our final.

### JAMES BOND V. TIGER

A solid start by the tiger as he paces around Bond, growling. But then James Bond pulls out a gun and shoots him. Why didn't Muhammad Ali think of that? I should point out that this was an *imaginary* final by the way, meaning that no tigers were harmed in this 'fight'. However, I accidentally forgot to follow this rule in the first round, so we *have* killed a lion.

Congratulations to James Bond, who now goes on to face Gandalf in the World Series. Gandalf came through a very tough group including Dumbledore, a shark and a pair of Ninja twins. Commiserations to all of our losers. Particularly the shark who can't even come to the after-tournament party.

# 90
# SHOULD YOU TELL SOMEONE THEIR GIRLFRIEND IS A NIGHTMARE?

Ah, glad you're here. Listen, we need to talk about Matt's girlfriend. Maybe we could use this chapter to do that and if Matt comes along we can all pretend we're just reading it like it's a normal chapter. OK?

Oh. My. God. That woman is a LIABILITY! You remember the first time Matt brought her along and no one knew who she was and then Matt said, 'Everyone, this is Fay,' and we were all, like, 'Aaah'? It was that time we all went out before Christmas last year – was it Dave's party? Yes! Dave's party at that Mexican place that's now a Nando's. God, that wasn't around for long. We quite liked her then, didn't we? I certainly did. She's quite pretty when you first meet her. But then she was very over-familiar with Dave and kept mussing his hair, do you remember? And she made those terrible comments about her gay neighbours in front of Simon and Claude. I know, I know, in her defence she was completely shit-faced but still. It was an early sign.

But she's done some odd things, though, old Fay, hasn't she? Remember when she made Matt take her home early from his birthday and his sister had come down from Hull specially and she wouldn't let him see her? What was that all about? And that skiing trip when she suddenly accused Jane, of all people, of not having any ambition, then said that every man she'd ever slept with had said it was the best sex they'd ever had? And that fight she almost started at the football? And what about the time she locked Matt out and he had to come and find us in his bare feet, wearing only the rubber foot-mat from his car? And the fire at the cricket club? That was *so* her who started it. And those Serbian guys she was trafficking in the back of that Movano last summer? What was all that about? And you know how she always wears too much make-up? Haven't you noticed? Look next time – there are mime artists who wear less foundation.

OK, OK, so we're agreed: Fay's a nightmare. What should we do? Should one of us maybe take Matt out for a drink and— Ah, I've just remembered, she doesn't let him go out for a drink with any of us any more unless she's there . . . Um . . . I know, perhaps someone should ring Matt at work and meet him for lunch and tell him gently what we all think about Fay . . .

Actually, no, I've just had a thought – not entirely sure where it's come from, to be honest, but here it is. We shouldn't say *anything* to Matt because Matt's not stupid: he'll eventually get himself out of Fay's clutches (unless, of course, he doesn't, and that will be because he likes being dominated by a strong-minded woman.* And in that scenario he'll really need friends around him – the kind of friends who haven't told him what they think of his girlfriend). The fact that other people's relationships may defy all logic is one of those eternal truths we all have to learn sooner or later, like the fact that you *can* be in it, but you *still* won't win it or that Father Christmas really does exist (see Chapter 23). 'Love is blind,' as Shakespeare put it, 'and lovers cannot see the pretty follies that themselves commit.' More to the point, *we* can't see what 'follies' the lovers themselves commit in the privacy of their bedroom. Perhaps that's where it all makes sense to Matt.

Bottom line? It's none of your business. I know people who still haven't forgiven their friends for telling them their girlfriends were a nightmare even when they subsequently chucked that girlfriend *for being precisely the kind of nightmare they were warned about.* So, are we all agreed? The rule is NEVER tell someone their girlfriend is a nightmare.

Just to be clear, though: if Matt ever brings it up in a conversation that he's having doubts about Fay, and you were to

..................................................................................

* Actually, that makes sense. Have you met Matt's mum?

give a very tactful indication that you may have your own *private* doubts, then that would be absolutely fine. But never, ever lead the charge.

Well done, everyone. Oh, and guys? Don't all leave this chapter at once or Matt'll wonder what we've been doing.

# 89

# ARE WE GOING TO LET RICHARD'S GEEKY WORDPLAY QUIZZES RUIN OUR CHRISTMAS AGAIN?

In 2012's *The 100 Most Pointless Things in the World* – still available in all good bookshops, and now additionally available in some terrible ones too (you know the ones I mean) – I set you three geeky quizzes, on US states, capital cities and Christmas number-ones. They were based largely on appalling puns and wordplay. The sensible among you will have quietly turned the page to read instead my trenchant opinion on wind chimes or some such.

But some of you took up the challenge and ruined your Christmas with endless family rows about Wisconsin or 'Bohemian Rhapsody'.

But you know what? If you weren't rowing about whether or not my clue for Idaho was shaky at best, you would have been forced to confront the real problems in your extended family instead. Now, I don't know what the specific problems of your extended family actually are, but I know for a fact that you don't want to be talking about them.

So let *me* ruin this Christmas, rather than Uncle Terry's liberal relationship with alcohol, or Nana Gwen's UKIP lecture.

Below are forty clues that will lead you to the names of forty UK cities. The clues are sometimes cryptic, sometimes puns, but always annoying. As a tip, I would print out a list of UK cities, as there are some surprising names.

Let's get on with the job at hand. Good luck, one and all!

1. USB Upgrade
2. Jamie's Feeling Better
3. Organ Bank
4. Continued
5. Home Of The Carchers
6. Lumpy Hot Stew
7. Definitely Not a Rip-Off
8. Björn, Benny, Agnetha And James
9. Cockney Chancellor
10. Two Clues
11. Run And Hide
12. City In Turkey Or Kenya
13. For All Your Trunk And Crate Emergencies
14. Leaver
15. Fire Queen

16. Buried S
17. Confusing For Lads
18. Cleats
19. Time To Move On To E
20. Funny Person I Follow On Twitter!
21. Replace Your Old Drugs
22. Genuine Caviar
23. Pan-Cook Rabbit Town
24. Mess Behind Rug
25. The Result Of A Chinese Burn
26. Dagenham?
27. Left Opening Around 1 September
28. A Right Tit
29. This City Won The Next One
30. This City Was Won By The Last One
31. Twirl Pasta In Silence
32. What I Did After I Gave Her An Undercoat
33. Lewis
34. Fish Porridge?
35. Hmm, Big Rain Storm
36. Disallows After Final Mix-Up
37. Witches Score
38. Ern Is
39. Aussie Bird Handler
40. Hidden Above

# HOW MANY COWS WOULD, THEORETICALLY, HAVE FITTED INTO MY CHILDHOOD BEDROOM?

Now, this book is not just about the big questions, like 'Does God exist?' and 'Which is the best crisp flavour?' We are also here as a valuable service to regular *Pointless* viewers who have arguments they would like us to solve. We're a lot like Jeremy Kyle in that respect.

One such plea came in via Twitter from Lucy Lappin. Lucy asks:

Dear Richard

Between 1975 and 1976 me and my brother shared a room which was probably about 8ft x 10ft. We frequently argued about how many cows could fit into the room. I said 8. He said 3.

I was only 4 in 1975 and had never seen a cow but I used to argue passionately that you could fit more than

3 into a bedroom. My brother refused to budge. Could I have been wrong?

We reminisced about 'the cow arguments' a couple of years ago but didn't actually resolve the matter.

It would be great if you could help.

I hope you'll agree that this is a perfect example of a pointless argument. Arguments between older brothers and younger sisters almost always are.

So, Lucy, and unnamed brother, here is y— No, wait a second, let's give your brother a name. I'm going to assume that parents who called their daughter Lucy in 1971 might have called their son Matthew. So, Lucy and Matt, here is your answer.

Your childhood bedroom has a floor space of 80 square feet. A grown Holstein- Friesian dairy cow is approximately 6 feet long by 2½ feet wide.

Here are the two ways we could stack those cows in your childhood bedroom. I should point out that no cows were actually harmed in the pointless imagining of this hypothetical situation. Though I did accidentally damage an imaginary bedside lamp.

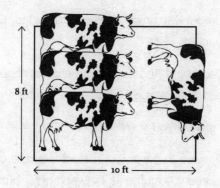

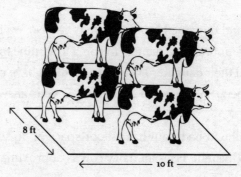

So, whichever way you want to do it, you and your brother could fit four full-grown dairy cows into your bedroom, which makes Lucy the loser. Congratulations, Matt, or whatever your name really is.

In the unlikely event that you've never had this specific argument yourself, we can draw one universal truth from it. If a younger sister has an unresolved childhood argument with an older brother, she should probably keep it to herself. Sorry, Lucy!

# 87

# IS EVERYONE EXCEPT ME AND MY FRIENDS AN IDIOT?

Here's the point: you and your friends *are* friends because you think alike. Where others may have gone with the Wanted, you and your friends totally went with One Direction. To you and your friends the question of what to do on Thursday night only ever had one answer: go and see a film, then have a curry.\* When you watch *Question Time*, you and your friends *love* what that man says (it's *exactly* what you would say if you were invited onto the show) and you get excited when his voice rises and he starts jabbing the table with his finger (it's *exactly* what you'd do if you were on the show), but you and your friends *hate* that other man, the one with the glasses who keeps shaking his head (who you'd 'accidentally' kick after the show, if you were on the show

......................................................................................

\* Actually, to be fair, you're not so narrow-minded as to have just one option. There's always the alternative where a late-night screening leads you to have the curry first, then see the film.

. . . which is just one of the reasons why you'll never be invited on).

In short, the world is divided into two vastly uneven categories: you and your friends, and everyone else. And it is absolutely beyond question that everyone except you and your friends is an idiot.

The only drawback is that, by the same token, *everyone* (except you and your friends) will be of the opinion that you and your friends are idiots.

Luckily that doesn't matter because, as you and your friends know, they are idiots.

# 86

## DO I HAVE TO GO TO BED WHEN MY MUM AND DAD TELL ME TO?

Here's an easy-to-hand chart to help you with this difficult issue.

| Age | Answer | Additional notes |
|-----|--------|------------------|
| 1 | Yes | . . . and no. Some high-pitched crying should get you out again. |
| 2 | Yes | Grrr, someone's been reading that 'Just leave it to cry' bollocks. |
| 3 | Yes | To be honest, quite knackered after playgroup, happy to kip. |
| 4 | Yes | Especially on Christmas Eve. Don't piss them off. |
| 5 | Yes | But this new word 'nightmare' seems to offer a little flexibility. |
| 6 | Yes | Makes sense if I want to be up by five to wake Mum and Dad. |

| 7 | Yes | But not when this whey-faced excuse for a babysitter tells me to. |
|---|-----|------------------------------------------------------------------|
| 8 | Yes | But it's not fair. It's not fair. It's not FAIR! |
| 9 | Yes | If only out of pity. The poor souls look like they regret having me. |
| 10 | Yes | Just found out the meaning of the word 'divorce'. |
| 11 | Yes | They were right: secondary school is a step up. |
| 12 | No | If I don't do my homework this time, it will be detention. |
| 13 | Yes | But I can only stay up till the end of what I'm watching. |
| 14 | No | I'm fourteen, for God's sake! No one tells me what to do. |
| 15 | Yes | Apart from Mum and Dad. Curse you, GCSEs. |
| 16 | No | But can you keep it down a bit? |
| 17 | Yes | Curse you, A levels. |
| 18 | No | I'm on my gap year, and I've not called home for weeks. |
| 19 | No | I'm at uni. Besides, the bar job doesn't finish till two a.m. |
| 20 | No | I'm at uni, in debt and there are no set hours in prostitution. |
| 21 | No | Curse you, finals. Wish I had Mum and Dad to send me to bed. |

| 22 | Yes | Back home, a new burglar alarm and they won't tell me the code. |
|---|---|---|
| 23 | No | Left home. Set up, new job, flat-share. |
| 24 | No | This is living. Inappropriate girlfriend, late nights, hangovers! |
| 25 | No | Moved in with better girlfriend. A lot of time in bed. Hubba hubba. |
| 26 | No | Engaged to girlfriend. Both work early mornings. |
| 27 | No | Bigger flat. Working hard. Sometimes I dream of bedtime. |
| 28 | No | Married to girlfriend. Some days I even see her. |
| 29 | No | Expecting our first. Can't wait. |
| 30 | No | Hooray! He's finally asleep. Let's have a drink. |
| 31 | No | Number two! Yay! (Come back, Mum and Dad, all is forgiven.) |
| 32 | No | Go to bed now, you two! Or no telly tomorrow. (Why am I threatening this? Telly is my only friend.) |
| 33 | No | Wish I was a child again, being looked after and sent to bed. |
| 34–50 | Ditto | ditto      ditto      ditto      ditto |

# 85
# ARE WOMEN FUNNY?

This is one of the simplest arguments in the book, and the actual answer need not detain us. Women are definitely funny.

But I've included 'Are Women Funny?' because it's a very useful debate. It's one of those simple tests of whether you're going to like someone or not.

Say you've just started working at a new office. You're finding your way, getting to know everyone. There's a guy who works in Marketing and he's kind of cute (he needs a haircut, but that's easily fixed) and you're starting to wonder if you should accidentally bump into him as he makes his morning cup of tea.

You then overhear him telling Gail from HR that 'Women aren't funny.' Hooray! He's an idiot! You never have to think about him again. Now, I bet that new temp with glasses knows that women are funny.

I've always been surrounded by funny women. Brought up by a family of them, dated them, employed them, been employed by them. I'm now the father of one, too. I'm sure most of you are the same. Some of you might even *be* funny women.

So, if you think women aren't funny I have bad news for you. They really are.

If women are never funny when you're in the room, then it's almost certainly because, for some unexplained reason, funny women feel uncomfortable around you.

Which is why you're at your desk talking about triathlons to Dave, while that new temp with glasses is laughing his head off with Sally in Pizza Express.

# 84

# DOES ALL MUSIC SOUND
# THE SAME THESE DAYS?

I remember my father saying that all pop music nowadays sounds the same. At the time we were listening to the chart run-down in the car on a family holiday in the eighties. That was a week when 'Bankrobber' by the Clash, David Bowie's 'Ashes To Ashes', Kate Bush's 'Babooshka', Bob Marley's 'Could You Be Loved', and 'Oops Upside Your Head' by the Gap Band were just some of the songs in the Top Twenty.

Obviously there will always be great music, and now, as much as at any time, people are writing properly excellent pop songs but, being completely honest, have you ever found yourself thinking – or saying – that it 'all sounds the same these days'? Below is a little test for you. In each pair of songs, one is a smash hit from the last two years and the other I have just made up. Can you spot the real ones?

# POINTLESS QUIZ

1. 'Don't You Worry Child'          'Gon' Make You Mine'
2. 'Need U (100%)'                   'Swear I'll Do Time'
3. 'Going Good To Firm'             'Mama Do The Hump'
4. 'On Da Corner'                              'Whistle'
5. 'Turn Around'                        'Fill The Hall Y'All'
6. 'Bucket'                   'Can You Hear Me (Ayayaya)'
7. 'Thrift Shop'                          'One 4 The Dads'
8. '(Gettin' A) Reputation'                    'Bom Bom'
9. 'Scream'                                   'Salute You'
10. 'International Love'     'Back Peddlin' (Same Old Joint)'
11. 'Fill Up'                                      'Ho Hey'
12. 'Only A Night And A Day'            'Sweet Nothing'
13. '212'                      'Kinda Means Yes (Right?)'
14. 'Truce'                               'Call My Name'
15. 'Hey Porsche'             'Hoo Shoo (Biddly Biddly)'
16. 'Attracting Flies'                        'Immature'
17. 'Miss Tuff It'                          'Ride Wit Me'
18. 'Down Boy!'                           'Hall Of Fame'
19. 'Latch'                               'Apothecarise'
20. 'Not Giving In'                           'Pon Da Us'

# 83

# HOW LONG IS 'TOO LONG' IN THE BATHROOM?

There are three times in life when you are allowed to spend a particularly long time in the bathroom.

1. Adolescence: 'That's four times he's washed his hair today.'
2. Early parenthood: sometimes going to the loo is the only peace you get all day. It is tempting to linger, isn't it?
3. Senior years: extra time allowed, to try to remember what you went in there for.

But outside these exceptions, how long should you spend in the bathroom? Or, more to the point of the argument, how long should your partner, kids or parents spend in the bathroom?

I have conducted a time-and-motion study with leading experts from the University of Imaginarychester, and these are our conclusions. Please photocopy this page and Blu Tack it to your bathroom door. Arguments solved.

### *MORNING*

*Mum* – fourteen minutes. Heaven only knows what you're doing in there, but you seem to smell nice and look nice when you come out, so take your time.

*Dad* – seven minutes. We all know you're not moisturising or exfoliating. How long does it take to clean your teeth, forget to floss and spray on some Lynx? You can have an extra two minutes if you still have hair that needs washing.

*Son* – one minute. Be honest, even that's a bit long.

*Daughter* – two minutes longer than your mum, because that new boy who looks like Max from the Wanted has started in your class.

*House guest* – as quick as you possibly can. Every second you're in there everyone is talking about how much you drank last night and wondering when you're going to leave.

*Builder* – it doesn't matter how long you take: no one's going in after you.

## EVENING

*Mum* – ten minutes. Except when you fancy a bath, in which case take two hours. Go on, be our guest – take every drop of hot water while you're at it. It's very important you don't drink that *entire bottle* of red wine too quickly. We've got your number, Mum.

*Dad* – as long as you can get away with. Everyone seems OK, don't they? It wouldn't do any harm to get your phone out and log on to that West Ham United forum. You haven't publicly given your views on the Hammers' defensive midfield weaknesses for some time. You know everyone else on the forum is sitting on the loo too? Wait! A knock at the door! Brush teeth quickly, then exit.

*Son* – one minute. Be honest, even that's a bit long.

*Daughter* – two hours, due to non-waterproof mascara, and the new boy who looks like Max from the Wanted asking Shelley if she wants to go to the cinema on Friday.

*House guest* – are you *really* still here? Exactly what is your definition of 'a couple of days'? If this goes on any longer, I'm going to have to wash your towel.

*Builder* – while I admire your work ethic, Stanislav,

you know British builders tend to knock off about four-ish?

## OVERNIGHT

*Dad* – it's all yours, buddy. Unless Stanislav needs the loo at some point.

## POINTLESS FACTS

In 1945, the German submarine U-1206 was sunk after the toilet malfunctioned, and a crewman's botched repair forced them to the surface. It was spotted and bombed.

Elvis is in good company – George II died on the toilet as well.

# 82 WHICH IS THE BEST POWER OF LOVE?

I know, you're looking at the chapter heading and wondering whether this is an authoritative discourse on qualities of love to be ranked alongside the meditations of C. S. Lewis or Søren Kierkegaard,* or whether it's an analysis of the more profound and universal question of which of the three number-one hits from the 1980s called 'The Power Of Love' is best. Well, this book doesn't shy away from the knotty and forbidding areas that other tomes might tiptoe around so you will not be surprised to learn that it is the latter. You want to learn about philosophy? Sorry, loser, this book's for people who've got all that stuff well and truly sorted. So, let's unpick and solve the argument that has held us in its thrall for the best part of thirty years.

......................................................................

* Having attempted to read the works of both Lewis and Kierkegaard, I'd recommend *The Lion, the Witch and the Wardrobe* way above *Frygt og Bœven*, unless you're fluent in Danish.

### *'The Power Of Love': Jennifer Rush*

Jennifer Rush was, incidentally, born Heidi Stern, but her record label didn't think that was a very good name for a pop star, even though 'Stern' happens to be German for 'star'. Still, they may have had a point with regard to 'Heidi', who, thanks to its literary associations, will always be a mildly irritating little girl from Switzerland.

This is the perfect eighties pop ballad, and an archetype of the form. Where would Berlin's 'Take My Breath Away' have been without this guiding hand at its back? A tremulous first verse over pulsing synths bursts into full-throated chorus, following the kind of four-square musical sequential melody a Pentecostal hymnist would be proud of – though said hymnist would no doubt blush at the kind of cheek-to-cheek, hand-to-arse dancing it inspired at the end of every disco. But little wonder we lapped it up. 'I am your lady,' assured Rush, 'and you are my man.' Fergie announced that it was Prince Andrew's and her favourite song and it was duly played *ad nauseam* around the time of the second biggest royal wedding of the decade.

### *'The Power Of Love': Frankie Goes to Hollywood*

This is another cracking song. It was a December number one for Frankie, although not actually a Christmas number one as it was knocked off the top slot by ruthless cash-in supergroup Band Aid. It's an interesting one, though, and a bit of a departure for Frankie as it was the first song they'd released that hadn't been banned for one reason or another ('Relax' was too saucy for radio, and the video for 'Two Tribes' had been too graphic for telly)** so there was a warm sense of the poachers turning gamekeeper whacked home by a video that remains the campest interpretation of St Luke on record. An ingenious string score adds direction and form to Holly Johnson's meandering verse but preps us for a chorus that rides in with more pomp and flourish than a Cecil B. DeMille epic. Disregarding the video's ongoing homage to *The Life of Brian*, this song is a monument to the arranger's art and succinct testimony to Trevor Horn's particular genius. Oh, and God's.

### 'The Power Of Love': Huey Lewis and the News
It's hard to think of a better rock song from the eighties. This one strutted into the charts like an unbeaten world wrestling champ in dressing-gown and silky shorts. I mean to say, when you're presenting the world with a supposedly new song, whose title has already been used to number-one effect not once but twice, the only attitude you can strike is one of total shameless brass neck. Along with its sister song, 'Jump' by Van Halen, it trimmed away the rough, somewhat yeastier edge of, say, the J. Geils Band and bound it up with bright, shiny synth stabs into a readily digestible rock lozenge for the eighties man (or woman) on the go. Huey himself, with his enviable collar-length eyebrows and twinkly

........................................................................................

** Obviously both could now feature on CBBC without a murmur.

American smile, seemed a fantastic sort of role model and the song's use in *Back to the Future* confirmed its place on the loftiest of eighties plinths.

I want to say that Frankie's was the best 'Power Of Love' as it's undoubtedly the coolest and hippest, but this book demands the truth so I have to impart that, for its utter confidence and total absence of cool, hipness and Fergie-connotation, the Huey Lewis 'Power Of Love' is simply the all-round better pop song.

So there it is. Which is the best 'Power Of Love'? It's by Huey Lewis and the News.

# 81
## WHICH IS BETTER –
## *POINTLESS* OR *THE CHASE*?

*Pointless.**

....................................................................................................

* We do love *The Chase,* though.

# 80

## WHO FARTED?

Humans are phenomenally well designed. Think about all the stuff we do. No, not just that stuff (although that is, to be honest, some of our best work), no, I mean just the normal stuff. We have irises that shrink in strong light and pupils that dilate when we see someone we fancy.* We have a mechanism in our throats that, like an old doorman at a masonic lodge, knows on instinct what to direct through the open passage and what to send down into the closed chamber below. We are properly awesome and this ingenious knack for engineering is shown thousands of times over in every one of us. Even better, like driving a car or using Sky+, we don't have to understand how it works, we just sit back and enjoy – unless the engine conks out or the bloody snooker overran. But nowhere is our design bettered, nowhere is the

...................................................................................

* Not always handy, especially if your spouse is standing nearby, watching your pupils.

flair and humour of whatever created us** more evident than in our fantastic trick of being able to float out noxious airs from our guts undetected.

Since the days when our ancestors wore skins and lived in caves, a time even before the very first Morse prequel, if you can imagine, humans have relished a good mystery to solve. And what with murders being comparatively rare in small Stone Age communities, the question of 'Who farted?' was the perfect opportunity for early man to further his quest for answers. Rough-hewn proto-Poirots would gather all their suspects in one of the larger (and better ventilated) caves*** and attempt to deduce from the collated evidence precisely who the culprit was.

The problem then, as now, is that farting is the perfect crime. Perfect in the sense that – except in very rare instances – no one dies, and perfect because the truly silent fart is impossible to pin on anyone (literally *or* metaphorically). The only evidence to work with is the reaction of the individuals when the crime is discovered. Some will colour, some will vehemently deny,

..............................................................................

** In debates between Darwinians and religious leaders, farting is seen either as the natural evolution of a digestive system responding to gaseous content or something God came up with after a few beers.

*** Libraries in private residences didn't become popular until the AD 1700s.

others still will accuse. If one person quickly leaves the room, they may well be the guilty party, especially if you then hear the door of the loo shutting. On other occasions the culprit will go on to reoffend and this, too, will significantly narrow the focus of blame especially if, emboldened by their first success, they throw caution to the wind and make a sound. However, most often the detective work will rest on instinct and hunch alone.

So, who farted? Aha, says the rookie sleuth. It was the one who went red! Who but the guilty one would feel embarrassed under such circumstances? But embarrassment can come from being thought guilty of a crime regardless of actual guilt. It is inconclusive. Maybe the person who pins the blame so readily is the guilty party – or the aloof person studiously not getting involved: as silent as their fart? The unsatisfactory truth is that, unless someone confesses to it, the mystery of 'Who farted?' will always remain unsolved.

Seeing as we all fart at some point, though, the blame is ultimately borne by every one of us equally. Therefore never send to know for whom the bell tolls . . .

Who farted?

It was YOU!

# POINTLESS FACTS

There is a town in Austria called Windpassing, in Niederösterreich, or Lower Austria.

The average fart is 59 per cent nitrogen, 21 per cent hydrogen, 9 per cent carbon dioxide, 7 per cent methane and 4 per cent oxygen – all essentially odour-less. Less than 1 per cent is what makes farts smell: minuscule amounts of ammonia, hydrogen sulphide and excrement, which can be smelt at one part per 100 million parts air, all wrapped up with traces of stinky hydrogen sulphide.

# 79
# SHOULD I WRITE A NOVEL?

Every middle-class person in Britain has one of the two following ambitions.

1. Write a novel
2. Set up an online cupcake business

Some people have both ambitions. In the next five years I bet there'll be thousands of novels about a semi-autobiographical hero attempting to set up an online cupcake business. Mine will be called *You Can't Make a Cupcake Without Breaking Hearts*.

But *should* you write your novel? You know the one I'm talking about. The one that's been following you around for a couple of years whispering, 'You know I could be a novel, don't you?' in your ear.

Well, the big trouble with this ambition is that writing a novel looks *quite easy*, but is, in fact, *really difficult*.

None of us says, 'My New Year resolutions are to lose a bit of weight, and maybe have a go at performing open heart surgery,' but we all think we can have a crack at a novel.

The main reason we think we can do it, is that writing *first lines* for novels is really, really easy. Do a couple now . . .

*The Ukrainian watched from a distance as Ryan walked that familiar road for the final time.*

Wait! *What?* Which Ukrainian? What do you mean the 'final time'? For the love of Christ, *someone warn Ryan*!

*The moon scuttled behind a cloud and something moved in the churchyard.*

OMG! *What* moved? Somebody warn whoever the *hero* is! Probably the *vicar*!

*As he exposed the two wires, knowing the lives of his entire platoon now depended on this one decision, Mulligan cursed his colour-blindness.*

It's a *bomb*! And Mulligan has to disarm it! And he's *colour-blind*! Hold on, why would a colour-blind guy be in charge of disarming a bomb? That doesn't ring true. Hmm. I hate it when it's Elaine's turn to choose at Book Club.

So, first lines are usually fun, and definitely easy. The trouble with writing novels is that everything *after* that is really difficult. In fact, other than the first line, the only fun things about writing a novel are thinking up names for the characters, and telling people in the office that you're 'working on a novel'. It's terrible to be told by someone in the office that they're 'working on a novel'. First, because you have to hear about it, but second, because they might actually *succeed*, which would destroy you. At least if someone's planning to set up an online cupcake business they bring in cupcakes.

Also, almost every single novel ever written fails in almost every way. The odds against you finishing are very high; the odds against an agent liking it are even higher; the odds against that agent selling it to a publisher are higher still, and the odds against anybody actually *buying* it when it's published are almost beyond comprehension. There are people in this world who never play the lottery because the odds of winning are not worth wasting a pound on. But they will happily spend three years sitting in a shed writing about a dystopian future society ruled by the souls of the dead, risking their marriage and their sanity, for precisely the same odds.

So, if writing novels is very, very, very hard and almost definitely doomed to failure, should you bother?

Of course you should!

Writing a novel is a particular type of dream, much like running a marathon. Just finishing it is enough in itself. It doesn't matter if no one ever reads it: you know you've written it, you know the places in your head you had to go into to write it, and you have, at least for a few months, dreamed the dream, and made your co-workers briefly nervous.

So, in the questions below, I bet you could have written all of the first lines. But if you think you could have written the novels themselves, then trust yourself and get on and do it. You will never regret it. But if your novel is called *Mulligan's Greenish/Purplish Berets* then I *will* sue.

Which novels begin with the following lines?

## POINTLESS QUIZ

1. I'd never given much thought to how I would die (2005)
2. Once there were four children whose names were Peter, Susan, Edmund and Lucy (1950)
3. Call me Ishmael (1851)
4. The sweat wis lashing oafay Sick Boy; he wis trembling (1993)
5. Mr and Mrs Dursley, of number four, Privet Drive, were proud to say that they were perfectly normal (1997)
6. This is the saddest story I have ever heard (1915)

7. Friday 15th July 1988, Rankeillor Street, Edinburgh (2009)
8. It was a bright cold day in April, and the clocks were striking thirteen (1949)
9. It was the best of times, it was the worst of times (1859)
10. No one would have believed, in the last years of the nineteenth century, that this world was being watched (1898)
11. I scowl with frustration at myself in the mirror (2011)
12. Sunday 1 January. 129 lbs (but post-Christmas), alcohol units 14 (1996)

# 78

## IS FATHER
## CHRISTMAS REAL?

You probably don't believe in Father Christmas. You know what? Fair enough. Hell, I don't believe in Louis Walsh. We all have these blind spots in our credos. Why do I assume you don't believe in Father Christmas? Well, for a start because you're reading this book. That is not to say *Pointless* appeals only to dour cynics who abjure dreamy childish fantasies – far from it. It was the indulgence of dreamy childish fantasies that actually got the show made in the first place (though I still don't know why the BBC commissioner made me dress as a nurse). It's just that if you're of an inclination to savour the kind of lofty and erudite back-and-forth that is the natural territory of a *Pointless* book, you probably think you've 'outgrown' believing in Father Christmas.

Nevertheless it is entirely possible that you may still wake up to some sort of stocking on Christmas morning.* There's something miraculous about how that thing that was just hanging limply last night is now bulging to the point of overflowing. And the same applies to the stocking. So, what is it exactly about a fat man with a beard climbing off his flying sleigh and entering your house via the chimney before heading on to dispatch presents to the beds of the rest of humanity during the hours of darkness between 24 and 25 December each year that sticks in your craw?**

I know what you're going to say. Someone at school told you that Father Christmas didn't exist when you were six (*six!*) and you've gone along with it ever since. Well, shall we just start by looking at some of the other things that 'someone at school' told you when you were six? You know Simon Wallis? He said Adam Ant was his postman. A bare-faced lie: his postman was Ray Jennings until 1987 and then it was Steven Pell, who was in fact also your postman. Jessica Branston said that her uncle was David Seaman. A figment of that same febrile Branston imagination that would later tell her boyfriend Alan Broughton that she'd been at a 5ive concert in Milton Keynes when in fact the only 'funk' she'd been 'slam dunking' that night was Jake Matthews's big brother's on a dirty stop-out. I could go on.

........................................................................

* I know I do.
** What are you? Fattist?

Is Father Christmas real? Let's be scientific about this and look at the evidence. Every Christmas morning billions of people all over the world wake up to find presents at the end of their bed. They all say it was Father Christmas. What are you saying? That every *single* parent in the world got together one day to sign up to a massive hoax that they all carry out to the last detail every December? *Every* parent? It's hard enough for Mum and Dad to agree with each other.

Is Father Christmas real? Is the Pope an Argentinian?

You know the best trick Father Christmas ever played? He's got us to do all his donkey-work for him. We buy the presents, guard them, lug them about, wrap them, and put them out exactly as he demands, covering his expenses and never expecting repayment. No wonder he's always laughing.

# HOW MANY TIMES CAN YOU REVISIT A BUFFET?

This is another of our viewer arguments. Gina Loizou asks whether her boyfriend is guilty of the age-old buffet crime of 'over-visiting'.

Gina writes:

This has been a source of much contention between my boyfriend and me for years.

How many times is it socially acceptable to revisit the free buffet after your first visit? Is it acceptable to revisit at all?

To answer that question we have, first, to discuss Buffet Psychology. I'm going to take as an example my local 'Chinese Buffet'. It is all you can eat for eight pounds. They'll then charge you two pounds fifty for a glass of water, but we're not falling for that, right? We're very happy to dehydrate, thank you.

Now, on the face of it, inviting hundreds of customers to eat everything they possibly can *without limit* and charging less than a tenner makes no financial sense. To be able to charge eight pounds the proprietors are relying on two things. And both are relevant to Gina's boyfriend.

1.  *The natural elasticity of the human stomach.* When we are hungry we imagine our capacity for food is almost infinite. You'll know this from the twelve-pack of Wotsits you bought last time you went around the supermarket while hungry. But the reality is that after, say, two large plates of reheated noodles and a series of unidentified things in breadcrumbs, most people imagine they will never need to eat again.

However, some people have stomachs that are, shall we say, *more elastic* than others. I'm going to assume that Gina Loizou's boyfriend is in this category. I'm not saying he's fat: he has, after all, managed to land himself a girlfriend, and one with a glamorous foreign-sounding name at that. But there are people capable of turning a lunch at the Chinese Buffet into the equivalent of a pub lock-in. And it is precisely because of these people that the buffet owners rely on their second weapon.

2.  *The natural shame of the human mind.* Fifty per cent of the population have a definite strategy to maximise their food intake at a buffet (you know the 50 per cent

I'm talking about). The real nutritional key is that if you don't overload on carbs too quickly your capacity to eat can be superhuman. This, of course, is why everything at the Chinese Buffet is covered with batter or breadcrumbs, and the only vegetables you can find are hidden deep within vast piles of noodles. But even the most enthusiastic overeating plan can be scuppered by shame. Some time around your third visit to the gleaming metal trays of battered prawns and popcorn chicken (just as an aside, we all know popcorn chicken isn't Chinese, don't we?), the brain of the average man notes the sweat that has begun to form on our upper lip. We then, unconsciously, suck our bellies in just that tiny bit, and maybe do an involuntary biceps flex. This is shame talking, and it's saying, 'Come on, Dave, remember you're going to do that triathlon this year. You've told everyone at work. Just have a pudding. Look, "fruit salad". Wow, that really doesn't look like a fruit salad.' Thanks, shame.

However, some people have a sense of shame which is, shall we say, *more elastic* than others. I'm going to assume that Gina Loizou's boyfriend is also in this category. I'm not going to say he's a sociopath: he has, after all, managed to find himself a girlfriend, and one who cares enough about him to seek solutions to his problems via the medium of a Christmas book spin-off of a popular tea-time quiz show.

But Gina's boyfriend is the worst nightmare of the buffet owner. A man with the elasticity of stomach and absence of shame to take 'all you can eat' literally. And in these circumstances the buffet owners have to rely on Gina to act as a natural brake.

So, to Gina's question. We know that her boyfriend will visit a buffet until concerned Greenpeace activists arrive to try to roll him back into the sea. But how many visits *should* he make?

I think, as human beings, we all instinctively know the answer. It's two big visits, one extra top-up visit because they've just brought out the sweet 'n' sour pork, and then a pudding. Anything more than that and you are officially out of control and your glamorous, quiz-show loving girlfriend is allowed to tut.

# 76
## RED OR BLACK?

Generations of gamblers have been drawn to the uncompli-
cated, straight up-and-down fifty:fifty offered by Red or
Black.* There's no need to shilly-shally with cards, work out
odds: it's just pure gambling jam with a spoon sticking out
of it; a betting proposition even a child could understand.

Did I say 'jam'? Well, that's as good a way to decide as any.
Red or Black?  Strawberry or blackcurrant? Which is it to
be? Strawberry sweeter, perfect on a scone with clotted cream.
Blackcurrant, tart, with a bit of a sting, the perfect wake-up
call with your breakfast croissant. How do you choose? Damn,
damn, damn – it's no easier with jam . . .

Red or Black?

..................................................................................

* Yes, well done, it's not quite fifty:fifty, is it? Thanks to the o (or
double o in Vegas). Glad you pointed that out.

Black or Red?

Red Nose Day – hooray!

Black Monday – boo!

Red good, Black bad.

Red it must be.

Or Black?

In the Red. In debt. Bad.

In the Black. In credit. Good.

Black it must be . . .

Or Red?

'Lady in Red': love it or loathe it, it's a hit. The lilting voice of Chris de Burgh, filling the dance floor with drunk divorcees-to-be.

'Lady in Black': Chris de Burgh's less successful follow-up about shagging a widow at her husband's funeral.

So, lady-wise, Red good, Black bad.

Red it must be.

Or Black?

It's a battle of Titans, two absolute equals. Red or Black, *yin* or *yang*, Chris Huhne or Vicky Pryce. A stark choice, compared to which, even the toss of a coin looks complicated. Heads or tails? Hang on, mate, how are you going to spin it? What, and then catch it and turn it the other way up? How dodgy is that? Wait, wait, wait, let's see the coin. Which is the head? See, there isn't a bloody head!  Another good reason not to join the euro . . .

There is, however, a definitive and 'correct' answer to the question 'Red or Black?' and it's this: 'Sod this pile of old toss. Let's see what's on BBC1.'

# ARE BANK HOLIDAYS A GOOD IDEA?

The big upside of bank holidays:

**YOU GET A DAY OFF WORK**

**THE BIG DOWNSIDE OF BANK HOLIDAYS:**

**EVERYBODY ELSE GETS A DAY OFF WORK TOO**

But, on balance, are they a good thing or a bad thing?

There are many different ways of solving arguments, but sometimes the best way is through the medium of poetry. By which I mean I have written a poem.

### *WHY BANK HOLIDAYS ARE BAD – A POEM*

The streets are packed
The shops are rammed
The trains are full, the roads are jammed.

You'll drive for miles
Then queue for hours
For Chessington or Alton Towers.

Or take the kids
To Hull or Crewe
Cos your family's got the day off too.

The beaches fill
With gals and fellas
Shelt'ring underneath umbrellas.

You know you hate them,
Every year.
So why not try out *this* idea?

Go to work!
Go on, just try it!
The perfect place for peace and quiet!

An empty office!
A sight so fine
Feel free to browse the *Mail Online*.

And you know you've always
Longed to use
That dryer in the ladies' loos.

Sleep at your desk,
And have no fear!
No one will see

No one can hear.
HR won't know,
You're in the clear!
iPlayer on
Ooh, look, *Top Gear*!
Water-cooler?
Fill with beer!
And all the while
Reflect with cheer
That your boss is sobbing in IKEA.

So, it's lovely to have eight extra days off each year, but wouldn't it be better if we could all *choose our own*? We could even tailor them to celebrate our own interests. For instance, I would take off 13 January (Stephen Hendry's birthday), 25 May (anniversary of the release of *Star Wars*), and 12 November (the day Julie is planning to bring her kids into work).

Below is a list of public holidays in other countries. Can you guess in which country each is observed? Incidentally, they have fifteen national holidays in Thailand. We only have eight! And it's hot over there.

## POINTLESS QUIZ
1.  Emperor's Holiday (23 December)
2.  Gandhi's Birthday (2 October)
3.  St Wenceslas Day (28 September)

4. Human Rights Day (21 March)
5. Bastille Day (14 July)
6. Chulalongkom Day (23 October)
7. Independence Day (4 July)
8. Koninginnedag (30 April)
9. Fiesta Nacional (12 October)
10. Unity Day (3 October)
11. Rose Of Lima Dau (30 August)
12. Waitangi Day (6 February)

# 74
# SHOULD I LEARN THE PIANO?

Andrew Lloyd Webber. Picture him. Now picture the beautiful women he has been associated with variously over the years. Well, what do you think? Do you ever, *ever* suppose that he would have got a look in if he hadn't learned the piano? Well? Should you learn the piano? Of course you should. What are you waiting for?

# 73

# DO YOU HAVE TO GO TO THE DENTIST EVERY SIX MONTHS?

I once had a date with a dentist. It went so well she asked to see me again in six months.

What is it with dentists and six months? You only have to MOT your car once a year, and surely your car is more complicated than your teeth? I mean, your teeth don't even have a crankshaft, or ABS as standard.

Don't get me wrong, dental health is obviously important. You will never see a dating advert that says, 'Would like to meet man, tall, 30–40, good sense of humour, no teeth.' But, really, are they all that hard to look after? Here is all the dental routine you will ever need.

Brush twice a day. Easy.

Floss once a day for 3–4 days in a row, then forget to

floss one day, then don't bother for a couple of weeks, then watch an item on *This Morning* about the importance of flossing, then floss once a day for 3–4 days in a row. Repeat.

Use mouthwash. Don't swallow, or you'll eventually end up in the park with a stray dog on a piece of string.

Don't eat too many sweets. Unless you really want to. They'll probably find out sugar is good for your teeth one of these days. Then just think about all the sweets you will have missed.

Don't box, or insult Glaswegians in pubs.

You know that if you go to the dentist in six months' time they'll root around in your mouth then say, 'All looks fairly good in there. I'd like to keep an eye on molar B7. Come and see me again in six months.'

Now let's say you leave it for *twenty years* before your next trip to the dentist. Then they'll root around in your mouth and say, 'OK, you probably should have visited me sooner. You have signs of decay in four or five of your teeth.'

You might think this sounds bad, but here comes the real genius of my plan. Because this is in twenty years' time, the next thing they say is: 'OK, let me just fire my newly invented, totally painless dentist laser at those teeth. One, two, three, four, five. OK, all fixed. Come and see me again in six months.'

So, do you need to go to the dentist every six months? No. Next, please!

## POINTLESS FACTS

In China, 20 September is Love Your Teeth Day.
The electric chair was invented by a dentist, Alfred Southwick from Buffalo, New York.

# 72

# ENGLISH FOOTBALL MASCOTS – BLESSING OR CURSE?

There are some things that will be for ever football: the roaring chants of the crowd, the fug of Bovril and meat-pie farts in the October twilight, the good-natured badinage of the terraces,* and the sight of grown men dressed head to foot in nylon animal costumes beating the crap out of each other on the pitch at half-time. Who can forget the Big Bad Wolf of Wolves taking on Bristol City's Three Little Pigs? That was in 1998 – and *still* their bitter property dispute rumbles on.

......................................................................................

* It is a fact that the NHS saves millions of pounds in anger-management therapy every year, thanks to out-patients finding emotional release in informing a man with a whistle that he is a self-abuser and telling the opposition's fans that they enjoy incest, to the catchy theme tune of *The Addams Family*. I shall be writing about this soon in the *Lancet*.

People tend to have two different reasons for disliking football mascots. Some will be the purists** who feel that football is going a bit Disney when it tries so hard to pander to families, while others simply wish their club had a different animal emblem*** from the one they have to watch doing lewd dances in front of the directors' box match after match. However, we at *Pointless* feel that the mascots of English football are among the finest features of our national game. We've even prepared a short quiz for you to test your mascot knowledge. Can you name the football clubs to which the following mascots belong?

## POINTLESS QUIZ

1. Pottermus
2. Barney the Owl
3. Monty Magpie
4. Deepdale Duck
5. Billy the Badger
6. Chirpy Cockerel

......................................................................................

** By 'purists' I mean, obviously, the kind of football fan who harks back to the good old days, when you wouldn't see mascots but genuine football fans fighting on the pitch.

*** They're not *all* animals, of course. West Ham, the Hammers, have . . . a hammer. A good, hard-as-nails, tough-guy mascot, befitting their proud East End roots. Almost enough to distract us from the fact that their other nickname, 'The Irons', has an unfortunate Cockney rhyming slang connotation ('iron hoof' = poof).

7. Gunnersaurus Rex
8. Mr Bumble
9. Stamford the Lion
10. Fred the Red
11. Gully the Seagull
12. Frogmore the Frog

# HOW DO YOU PRONOUNCE...?

There are lots of arguments about exactly how to pronounce lots of very common words. Let's deal with them all here.

### 'SCONE' OR 'SCONE'
The answer is 'scone'.

### 'BOWIE' OR 'BOWIE'
This is an easy one. It's 'Bowie'.

### 'EITHER' OR 'EITHER'
It is 'either'. By which I don't mean either is correct. Just 'either'. The same goes for 'neither' v. 'neither'. 'Neither' is correct, but which I also mean that 'neither' is incorrect.

### 'GARAGE' OR 'GARAGE'
There are arguments for both, but we have to choose one so I'm going with 'garage'.

## 'SHREWSBURY' OR 'SHREWSBURY'

People from Shrewsbury go nuts if you pronounce it 'Shrewsbury', so please, please, please, call it 'Shrewsbury'.


## 'URANUS' OR 'URANUS'

Let's talk through 'Uranus' for a moment. You'd think 'Uranus' would be fairly simple to clear up, but instead the sound of 'Uranus' is always getting you into trouble. The correct pronunciation is, of course, 'Uranus'. I would ask all of you to spread the word. Commuters: talk loudly about 'Uranus' on a crowded train. Teachers: please tell your class about 'Uranus' in great detail. Single men: discuss 'Uranus' as an ice-breaker on your next blind date.

And, while we're at it, the Harry Potter books were written by J. K. 'Rowling' not 'Rowling'.

You buy your trainers from 'Nike' and 'Adidas', not from 'Nike' and 'Adidas'.

Your headache tablets are 'paracetamol' not 'paracetamol', and 'ibuprofen' not 'ibuprofen'.

In a celebrity-run restaurant Jake 'Gyllenhall' would serve you 'scallops'.

I hope I've cleared up any 'controversy' about 'pronunciation' way ahead of 'schedule'. For the sake of your 'privacy' please put this page in an 'integral' 'envelope'. I wouldn't want to give you a 'migraine'.

# 70

## IF YOU COULD ONLY EAT ONE FOOD FOR THE REST OF YOUR LIFE WHAT WOULD IT BE?

Imagine you're trapped in a warehouse and setting foot outside is absolutely out of the question for maybe twenty, twenty-five years. If you've ever got lost in IKEA for twenty, twenty-five minutes, you'll have some idea of the warehouse claustrophobia you will suffer. Or, to be less specific, you're in there at the very least until, say, radiation levels have dropped sufficiently or Ann Widdecombe has finished her pantomime run at the local theatre. For the sake of argument, we'll say there is a small galley-style kitchen with a toaster and a basic oven in the warehouse and a water-cooler with several thousand massive bottles of the clear stuff. Maybe water-cooler water is one of the two things that are stored at this particular warehouse.* The other thing is a single type

...........................................................................

* The water-cooler provides an added bonus: as madness sets in, you'll have a great place to go to when you feel like talking to yourself.

of food and this one food is therefore the only thing you will eat quite possibly for the rest of your life. What would that food be?

| | |
|---|---|
| Crisps | Nice for a bit but then they're just too potato-y. And crispy. And, as time passes, stale-y. |
| Toast | Nah. Think about it: whatever you spread it with, it's going to get boring after three meals. And, actually, you have nothing to spread on it. Forget it. |
| Baked beans | Consider the steady build-up day after day of bean gas. And then, twenty-five years on, when they come to rescue you, one spark and the explosion will be heard for miles around. Still, on the plus side, you'll be long dead before then. |
| Chicken | Mm, we love chicken. But for ever? Surely the ultimate torture. It'll just get you thinking . . . roast potatoes, stuffing, gravy . . . Or tonight a *coq au vin*. No, dammit, it has to be *coq au* water-cooler water. Which, let's face it, is basically *coq*. |
| Nutella | Come on now, don't be silly. A bit nutty. And what if you develop an allergy? |
| Baked potatoes | Well, if we thought crisps were too potato-y . . . |
| Pot Noodle | Most promising item so far but likely to |

become a chore after a couple of weeks, three times a day . . . It would have to be just one flavour – and which would you go for? All the same, there are other 'bits' in it, which look vaguely like food. You could, say, save up all the 'red bits' and, as a special treat, have a meal of pure 'red bits'.

Frosties
Oh, yes, there's also a milk cow stranded with you in the warehouse. I forgot. Even so I can't see Frosties working beyond the second day. You'd be craving some sort of meat. Still, let's think this menu through . . .

| Day 1 | Frosties with milk |
| Day 2 | Frosties with milk |
| Day 3 | steak |
| Day 4 | Dry Frosties |
| Day 5 | steak |
| Day 6 | Frosties and water-cooler water |
| Day 7 | steak |

Hm . . . a contender.

Fray Bentos
The famous tinned steak and kidney pie, with the oddly appealing sub-crust that resembles a damp grey cloth. You know what? That doesn't sound half bad, does it? For variety's sake you could have it underdone for breakfast so the pastry's nice and soft and then crispy for supper.

But now I'm starting to worry about the strong meaty flavour (assuming it *is* meat in there . . . and my lawyers have assured me that I should most certainly assume it). That's going to pall towards the middle of the second year.

Pop Tarts | I don't think you've thought this through. It's a marathon not a sprint.

Marathon | So this place is a depository for old-fashioned Snickers bars? I wondered where they'd all gone to. Well, there's plenty of variety in there: salt, sugar, nuts, chocolate – ooh, that's a front-runner for sure. But you can't just live on sweets: it'd do things to your head. Wouldn't it? And you'd also get very, very spotty.

Sprint Bar | Oh, you said *not* a Sprint. Sorry.

Cheese | On its own, cheese would drive you mad – the biscuit cravings would get too much.

Lasagne | Be honest, how fond are you of horsemeat?

Spag bol | If this is from a tin, ditto.

Chicken soup | You may be the person who proves that it's not so good for the soul after all.

Fish fingers | Now hang on, this is beginning to sound like a plan. Oh, boy, crispy golden breadcrumb, soggy fish – *yin* and *yang* – the ultimate comfort food.

It's becoming clear now. Here, without doubt, is the winning order.

1. Fish fingers
2. Frosties (+ cow)
3. Pot Noodle

Nuclear war, Ann Widdecombe, I'm ready for you now. Take me to Captain Birdseye's warehouse!

# 69

# IS BEING A BASSIST A PROPER JOB?

My brother is a bassist. That is his job. He gets paid for plucking four strings (I think it's four strings: I'm not the musical one in the family).

My job, meanwhile, is spending forty-five minutes every weekday telling people that Patagonia isn't a country and making puns about mountains.

So, pity my poor mum who, long ago, gave up any hope that her sons would have proper jobs.

Simply to convince my mum that being a bassist *is* a proper job, here are fourteen famous bassists. (And, yes, there *are* fourteen famous bassists – well, thirteen famous bassists and whoever Mike Dirnt is), each of whom has made an actual living from playing a bass guitar. Sorry, Mum.

Can you name the band with which each enjoyed their greatest chart success?

## POINTLESS QUIZ

1. Sting
2. John Deacon
3. Guy Berryman
4. Gene Simmons
5. Dougie Poynter
6. Adam Clayton
7. Mike Dirnt
8. Geddy Lee
9. Paul McCartney
10. John Paul Jones
11. Roger Waters
12. John Entwistle
13. Christopher Wolstenholme
14. Flea

# 68

# WAS SHAKESPEARE THE BEST WRITER EVER?

This one was sent to us by James, and it's an argument he often has with his dad. Was Shakespeare the best writer ever?

There have always been story-tellers – many of whom were 'writers' (as in they made stuff up) without necessarily being 'writers' (as in literate), a distinction that still holds good with regard to tabloid journalists. There has – particularly in the Celtic strongholds of Britain – always been a custom of bards and poets passing on tales from generation to generation by word of mouth, an oral tradition that has been with us for thousands of years. Your job as storyteller was a deceptively simple one: to entertain and occasionally thereby to educate. So when our ancestors sat around the fire at the end of the day it will have been the good storytellers who were asked again and again to speak up while the bad storytellers would quickly have been assigned other duties, like arranging the rocks around the fire or reviewing the good storytellers. But the contract between 'writer' and audience has always been the same: entertain us and we will listen/read/buy your mini-series when it comes out in a box-set. Throughout every generation of humanity this is how good storytellers have become renowned. Of all the discoveries you make in your teens, the loveliest – all right, second loveliest – is that all those old books that you've heard people banging on about and dreaded picking up are actually cracking reads. Or beautifully written. Or, goddammit, both. Leaf through* Dickens, Hardy, Austen, Thackeray or, in fact, any famous author's work and you soon realise that these authors are actually famous because a critical mass (in every sense of the phrase) of people *loved* reading them.** Not teachers, not sado-masochists, just people.

Shakespeare was a peerless storyteller. In fact, he was so good that some people still claim he didn't actually write his plays: they're so damned good that someone else, far cleverer, must have written them. (You don't hear that said

........................................................................................

* Kindle-users and the like will, of course, 'click through' rather than 'leaf', but I would still recommend having at least one classic work in paper form, if only as a useful place to store an old postcard, which you'll use as a bookmark and come across decades later, prompting a flood of memories. The Kindle 'bookmark' does not do this.

** The exception to this rule is probably James Joyce. Yes, he's famous, but he's mainly famous for being a tricky old bugger to understand. So, you might want to hold off from reading him for a bit. Or a lifetime.

when the latest Jeffrey Archer novel comes out.) He crafted intrigues and injustices that you simply have to see worked through (think of Rounds 1 and 2 of a normal episode of *Pointless* and you're not far off it); he gets his villains and heroes – much like I do our pairs of contestants in a *Pointless* head-to-head – to do their thinking out loud to make it more fun, and his comic turns, though sometimes laboriously witty after the Elizabethan style, show a genuine comedy writer's genius (again, think of Richard's summing up at the end of each *Pointless* round and you're pretty much on the money).

Don't be put off by the poetic language – for heaven's sake, there are One Direction songs I don't fully understand but I'm happy to let the general gist wash over me. ('Shall I compare thee to a summer's day? Thou art more lovely and more temperate . . .'; 'That's what makes you beautiful'. Of course, the two lyrical works flow seamlessly together – they both draw from the same well, the same dark, mysterious and strangely odoured depths we mere mortals call 'genius'.) Nor should the fact that Shakespeare is something that's thrust upon you at school be allowed to colour your judgement. He was the first prolific writer in our culture to have had his works printed *and* given as an essential freebie to every castaway on *Desert Island Discs*, he shaped our very language***

........................................................................................

*** So many phrases we use to this day were first coined by Shakespeare. You might say that's neither here nor there. But then you'd be quoting from *Othello*.

and – some would argue – our earliest understanding of psychology, while his poems and plays remain the high-water mark of English literature four hundred years after his death.

I'm not saying he needs to be your favourite writer of all time, but was Shakespeare the best writer ever? Damn right he was.

Oh, and while we're here, let's sort out another question for you.

To be or not to be?
To be.

---

## POINTLESS FACTS

Shakespeare had seven siblings and two of them were called Joan.

Suicide occurs an unlucky thirteen times in Shakespeare's plays.

Two of Shakespeare's plays, *Hamlet* and *Much Ado About Nothing*, have been translated into Klingon. The Klingon Language Institute plans to translate more!

# 67

# WOULD YOU HANG AROUND WITH YOUR RELATIVES IF YOU WEREN'T RELATED TO THEM?

Let's take it as a given that we love our families. Even Uncle Keith has his uses, such as when we need to be able to describe the inside of a prison cell for our sociology homework, or if we want Jeremy Kyle's autograph. But would they actually be our *friends* if we weren't related?

This argument is simply solved with a quick hypothetical.

Picture the scene. You walk into your local pub on any normal Thursday evening, expecting to see your friends. But something isn't right: Big Dave isn't propping up the bar in jeans built for a much younger, slimmer man (in fact, himself twelve years ago), Kellie and Shelley aren't discussing whether, at gunpoint, they would rather sleep with Simon Cowell or Louis Walsh, and Quiz Tony isn't trying to pull a bemused Danish au pair by reeling off every FA Cup-winning team since 1959. Where have your *friends* gone?

You scan around the bar, and at your normal table, near the dartboard, instead of the regular faces, you see a group of total strangers. Confused, you sit down and idly make conversation, only to be immediately faced with a woman thirty years your senior who looks disappointed every time you casually swear and wishes you'd had a shave before coming out. She also looks alarmingly like you.

Next you meet Simon, an older, more successful version of yourself that the woman seems very proud of for some reason. She keeps asking why you aren't more like him. After a couple of pints to settle your nerves, the woman gets a bit personal and asks why you haven't settled down like Simon before she spirits a couple of toddlers from the ether and forces you to play peek-a-boo with them for about an hour while the others smile and take pictures.

You look around the table: you see a teenager, who plays on his phone throughout everything, and a motorbike-obsessed man, pushing seventy, who keeps insisting that Formula 1 isn't 'real racing', regardless of what everyone else around the table happens to be talking about. He never gets a round in.

After three drinks a huge argument breaks out about a holiday to the Lake District in 1983, and they all leave, taking you with them. It's 7.30 p.m.

Quick hypothetical ends. I hope it wasn't too subtle for you?

So, by and large, we're happy and blessed to have a loving and lovely family but, no, we would not hang around with our relatives if we weren't related to them. Say what you like about Big Dave, but he never wets a hanky and dabs the corner of your mouth with it.

# 66

## AM I PSYCHIC?

I would love it if some people really were psychic. Think about it: wouldn't life be so much more interesting if we could believe in a completely separate sphere of existence that ran alongside ours? A world of ghosts, of accurate predictions and the explaining of weird coincidences, such as when *exactly* the same word appears at the end of the first and third sentences of a paragraph about people being psychic. But, Xander, I hear you say (actually, it's a voice inside my head . . .), what are you talking about? Life is interesting enough, thank you very much, with its evolving nature, its loves, its births and deaths, its turbulent history and its daily tea-time quiz shows on BBC1. What do you take us for? Children? Well, you know what? You're right. Life really has given us plenty to be going on with.

But, still, it would be cheering, wouldn't it, to think that there was more to the whole experience than just the bits where we burble, crawl, walk, hobble, burble and then keel over? I would like desperately to believe in the supernatural. My only problem with it is the people who do believe in the supernatural. Every time I see a woman* of a certain age with furiously bobbed hair and an unshakeable conviction that she can commune with invisible people known only by initials, another little string of the cord from which my disbelief is suspended pings and the whole system looks more and more like it's about to come crashing down to Earth.

But then we always rehang our disbelief even if only by a thread because, as I think the Archbishop of Canterbury once said, the kind of supernatural we're happiest to engage with is the kind that we readily acknowledge is almost certainly bollocks.** We're much more comfortable not having to believe in it, but we still like to have it there so that when inevitable coincidences happen in our lives we can draw a strange, bogus comfort from them, think, Oooh, and move on. Some of you reading this will have thought that very thing.

Yes, the very same thing.***

..................................................................................................

* I say 'woman', it could possibly be a man, though frankly I'd find a man with furiously bobbed hair even harder to take seriously.
** It may not have been the Archbishop of Canterbury, it could have been Scooby-Doo. Or maybe someone who's dead now. If only they could give us some kind of sign, like, say, a claim for copyright infringement.
*** Oooh.

Why do 'psychics' always speak in riddles? Maybe because they themselves don't know the answer. So they keep blundering onwards, tying themselves in knots that will never resolve themselves, like scriptwriters on *Lost*. More likely, though, it's because the curious world they inhabit functions for us only as a mystery. If they were clear and concise we'd all be scared at how mental they were and would run away. And at the other extreme, if they ceased to exist we'd all have lost a strange but compelling harmonic from our lives.

So, are you psychic?

There's only one correct answer and it's 'Oooh, maybe . . .'

## POINTLESS FACTS

Medium Doris Stokes sent invitations to people who she had researched and placed them in reserved seats at her 'hearings'. From *The After Death Experience*, Ian Wilson (1987).

# 65

## DOES REPEATEDLY PRESSING THE BUTTON FOR A LIFT MAKE IT COME QUICKER?

No, it never has and it never will. It's still fun to do, though.

# 64
# WHICH IS THE BEST BREED OF CATTLE?

This is one that rages around breakfast tables up and down the country: which of the many types of cow is best? There are so many uses for cows* – milk, meat, suet, weather forecasting, leather, pulling things, and even in their downtime just standing around in fields looking so damn sexy** – but which cow gives the best all-round performance? There are those Friesians – the black and white ones (which also cost less to own as the licence is cheaper), Aberdeen Anguses, Jerseys, Longhorns, Guernseys, Highland, Kobe, Ayrshire and Belted Galloway to name just a few off the top of my head.

Most cattle take their names from their breeding grounds, much like hereditary peers. For instance, the Aberdeen Angus is so called because they initially hailed from the Scottish

......................................................................................

* I *know*! Who knew?
** Oh, come on, let's not have this argument again.

counties of Aberdeenshire and Angus. I explain this for any of you who may have thought it was perhaps a breed from Aberdeen, where every single animal has the first name Angus. That would, of course, be very silly. The cows would get confused as to which Angus they're gossiping about or which Angus has just been called across the field by, well, Angus. Identity fraud would be rife. And, besides, why would any self-respecting cow have a *boy*'s name?

Kobe is a district in Japan, famous for its Kobe beef. The meat from Kobe cattle is seen as a finely marbled delicacy, created in part by including beer in the cattle's diet. 'Kobe beef' . . . How exotic that sounds, compared to 'pissed cow'. If you like the sound of a cow that gets legless before it's made legless, Kobe is the beast for you.

The Longhorn is not named after its place of origin. It's named after the length of its horns, which have been described by experts as 'long'. There are two main kinds of Longhorn, the English Longhorn and the Texas Longhorn, both of which *are* named after their place of origin, which makes me momentarily want to rethink the first sentence of this paragraph. You know what? It's fine. The English Longhorn has a white patch along the length of its spine and running under its belly – it's the closest Nature can come to telling a butcher, 'Cut along this line.' The horns of English Longhorns generally curve in towards their faces, unlike the Texas Longhorns, whose horns are bigger, jutting out far more directly and measuring up to eight feet from tip to tip. The Texas Longhorn is the only breed of cattle that refers to English Longhorns as Shorthorns.

You'll be pleased to hear there is a clear winner here and it is the Gloucester. They are beautiful cattle, chocolatey brown with a white belly. They are impeccably behaved (great with children), delicious (great with horseradish), very strong for pulling stuff around, and their milk is famous for its cheese (Single and Double Gloucester *and* the renowned Stinking Bishop).

Double Gloucester is the cheese used for the annual race at Cooper's Hill, where untrained enthusiasts, known locally as 'idiots', tumble down an insanely steep gradient after a rolling cheese. Limbs have been broken. Sometimes, even, someone loses consciousness, but not for long – who needs smelling salts when you've got the Stinking Bishop on hand?

Below are some breeds of cattle with alternate letters removed. Can you name the following?

# POINTLESS QUIZ

D_O_G_T_A_T_R

H_G_L_N_

D_X_E_

B_L_I_N_ _L_E

H_R_F_R_

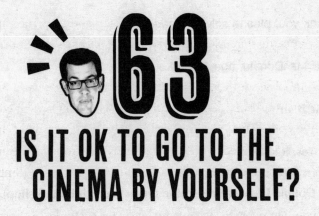

# IS IT OK TO GO TO THE CINEMA BY YOURSELF?

It is always nice when you can genuinely change someone's life for the better. This was one of the problems we received when we asked *Pointless* viewers to send us their arguments.

Dear Richard & Alexander,

My argument is with my friends and apparently society. Is it acceptable to go to the cinema alone?

Apparently there is an unwritten rule that it is creepy to do so. However, Don Draper from *Mad Men* (coolest man alive) frequents the cinema alone. So . . . Is it acceptable to go to the cinema alone?

Please note, I do have many people to go to the cinema with, it was just one occasion I almost went alone but couldn't bring myself to face the shame.

Thank you, please solve this debate.

Blair MacDonald, age 19 and a half

Dear Blair

1. Yes, it's OK.
2. In fact, it's awesome.
3. In fact, it's just about the single most grown-up thing you can ever do. Except for wearing cufflinks.
4. Whenever you go to the cinema by yourself, when you walk in you will see other people going to the cinema by themselves dotted around. You all unspokenly understand that you are doing something cool.
5. You get all the pick 'n' mix.
6. No one says, 'Isn't he the guy from before? The one who had the gun?' during the good bits.
7. Everybody knows this, Blair.
8. Therefore your friends are idiots.
9. So, if you take my advice, you should find some new friends.
10. And then *not* go to the cinema with them.

# 62
# AM I ENTERTAINING WHEN DRUNK?

Are you entertaining when you're drunk? Hmm. Well, how can I put this? You're *interesting* when you're drunk, I'll certainly go that far, and, yes, you give all of us something to talk about. Quite often, even when you're not there, we'll pass the time discussing, very affectionately, what you're like when you're drunk, and that *is* entertaining.

The truth is, you relax when you've had a drink and that's nice, but let's be honest, 'relaxing' does different things to different people. Some people are certainly better company when they've relaxed a bit. But it's that 'a bit' part that's key. You see, your problem is – no, not 'problem', I don't want to give the wrong impression here – your *crisis* is that you feel a bit better after a couple of drinks so you calculate that you'll feel a lot better after lots of drinks. I can't fault your logic there but these are actually two different lines on the graph. The lines? Well, you could say they're sort of 'your relaxedness' and 'other people's relaxedness'. Hell, it may be that you do feel lots better after lots of drinks it's just that, well, you become quite strident. Just a bit – and more often than not you can get a bit cross. And again, on one occasion, *that* was entertaining, genuinely entertaining, it really was, but for much of the time it's just quite wearing. The bit where we have to frogmarch your dead weight through kebab queues in town centres while you swear and take swings at us probably tickles the constables on late night patrol but let's just say it's not *The Last of the Summer Wine* for us.

Are you entertaining when you're drunk? No. No you're not.

# 61
# IS IT BETTER TO BE GOOD-LOOKING OR CLEVER?

We all know clever people: they're the people we take our tax returns to, or they're Daphne from *Eggheads*. And we all know good-looking people. They're the ones whose Facebook profile we're looking at when our partner comes in unexpectedly. But which would we rather be?

Of course, some people are good-looking *and* clever, such as George Clooney or Rachel Riley off *Countdown*. And some people are neither good-looking *nor* clever, but they can still go on to have a very happy and healthy career presenting *Piers Morgan's Life Stories.**

But let's say you *have* to be one or the other: which gives you the biggest advantage in life? I have broken 'Good-looking

...................................................................................

* I have met Piers Morgan and, annoyingly, he's actually quite clever. And, even *more* annoyingly, he was really nice.

v. Clever' down into a series of ten facts and given scores for each:

1. Every clever person secretly wants to be good-looking. But most good-looking people couldn't give a toss about being clever. Perhaps if they were cleverer they *would* give a toss, but they're not so they don't. *Good-looking* 8 *Clever* 2

2. A good-looking person can sleep with Justin Timberlake, while a clever person can tell you that an anagram of Justin Timberlake's name is 'I'm A Jerk But Listen!' *Good-looking* 9 *Clever* 4

3. Being clever can often help you with being *funny*. And being funny is the only thing that can match being good-looking in dealings with the opposite sex. It is possible to 'laugh someone into bed', but very difficult to 'discuss Einstein's law of thermo-dynamics someone into bed' or 'outline the objections you have recently made to your local planning authority concerning your neighbour's side-extension someone into bed'. Being good-looking *and* funny is very rare, and sensationally annoying when it happens (I'm looking at *you*, Jack Whitehall). Being clever and *not funny* is also fairly rare, but is very dangerous because it forces you to take life very seriously indeed (you often see it in politicians or extremists). *Good-looking* 3 *Clever* 9

4. If you're clever you can, with a bit of effort, get anything you want. But if you're good-looking you can,

with no effort whatsoever, get anything you want. *Good-looking* 10 *Clever* 7

5. If you're good-looking you're more likely to be in *Hollyoaks*. *Good-looking* 0 *Clever* 10

6. If you're good-looking you're more likely to become a film star, a rock star or a model. If you're clever you're more likely to be an accountant for a medium-sized agricultural-machinery-parts company in the West Midlands. Though there are *more jobs* for clever people. For example, it takes a lot of people to conceive, design and build a new car, but only one person to lie on its bonnet in a swimsuit at a trade show. *Good-looking* 8 *Clever* 4

7. If you're clever you can become a doctor. If you're good-looking you can marry a doctor. Net salary identical, but seven years less training. *Good-looking* 8 *Clever* 5

8. If you're good-looking you can win *The X Factor*. If you're clever you can win *The Voice*. *Good-looking* 5 *Clever* 5

9. Being good-looking is a big advantage in court. Scientific studies have shown that juries are far more likely to acquit defendants who are good-looking. And a study at Cornell University also discovered that, even if they were convicted, good-looking defendants received sentences twenty-two months shorter than someone less attractive. But, on the other hand, if you were *really* clever you wouldn't have got caught in the

first place. *Good-looking* 8 *Clever* 5

10. Good-looking people are less likely to be able to complete a Sudoku. Clever people are less likely to be invited onto a yacht full of models by a Russian oligarch. *Good-looking* 5 *Clever* 5

So, we simply have to add those numbers together to find out if it's better to be good-looking or clever. And it's fairly obvious to see the clear winner is goo— No, wait, hold on a second. If you're clever you'll already, as a matter of course, have added the numbers together, but if you're good-looking you won't have bothered (who needs numbers with *those* cheekbones?).

So the winner, by 74 points to 19, is . . .

CLEVER!**

......................................................................................................

** Ssssssh!

# 60
# IS MY WIFE CHEATING ON ME?

So let's go over what you've told us. You have for some time now suspected that your wife is cheating on you, is that right? You say she 'doesn't really talk' to you any more, and that the fact you never listen is beside the point. What matters is the semblance of communication. You say that she spends most of the time texting or tweeting 'some other person or people'? Apparently it's unsettling that she does it so often, whereas *you* only text people when it's urgent or work or, if I heard you right, 'quality banter'. She goes out a lot on her own to see 'girl-friends' for dinner, quite often coming home late. She will often leave the room – on one occasion, the house – to make or receive phone calls. The volume at which you were playing Tangerine Dream's *Greatest Hits* was, you are adamant, *not* the issue. And you've heard how easily she can lie in the past because you've heard her making up brilliant and credible excuses to other people. That one about cricking her neck while recharging her Kindle was worthy of a BAFTA.

OK, anything else? Oh, yes, she's started to wear a bracelet that was a present from 'one of the other mothers at school'. But it can't be an affair with another woman because she isn't . . . well, you know . . . When you suggested that she and Zoë might like to join you in . . . Yes, you did tell me about that.

Anything else I've missed? OK, and you want to know if she's cheating on you. No, she's not. Emphatically not. It's all, like that thing with her and Zoë, in your head. Oh, there's more? You looked out of the window one night when she was being dropped off at home and saw 'someone's car' driving off? Well, OK, OK, sit down. Please sit down. I can't concentrate with you pacing around like that.

Let's be absolutely clear. Your wife is *not* having an affair. She is suffering from having a husband who thinks she is having an affair. Of course, she may not know that's the direction your mind is going in. All she knows is that you've become very grumpy and – please sit down – withdrawn. Actually, before we continue, when did you last have a shower? No, no, not *that* obvious. Sure, you've been a bit down, I know . . . But no wonder she feels more comfortable talking to other people at the moment. Jeez, right now so would I. No, it's nothing personal. Hang on, let me rephrase that – of course it's bloody personal! Why is she not going out with *you* for dinner? Why is she free all these evenings to see girlfriends? Is it, I have to ask, vital that you watch every *single* game of football in Europe?

Your wife is not cheating on you. You have to recognise and convince yourself of that. You're poisoning your own mind, pissing in your own soup . . . Or Pot Noodle, yes, if that's what you've been eating lately. But listen: she is not. Cheating. On. You. All those things you mentioned that you think amount to evidence? Circumstantial at best; each and every one is utterly plausible on its own terms. Even Hercule Poirot gets it wrong sometimes – they just never show those ones on telly. But if you start thinking your wife is cheating on you, then she might as well be because the corrosive thought process has already begun. Right up until the very moment when you actually catch us *in flagrante*, she is uh . . . uh, she's, um, what was I saying? Um, she's innocent. You hear me? I hope that's put your mind at ease. If anything, mate, you should give her more space.

# 59

# WHAT SHOULD I CHANGE MY NAME TO?

We've pretty much all got boring names. Everyone at my school was called Richard, Mark, Matthew, Simon, Nick, Emma, Claire, Louise, Laura or Joanne. And everyone at my kids' school is called Jack, Harry, Ryan, Billy, Chloë, Maisie, Ellie or Poppy. Statistically *you* are probably called Stephen Collins or Katherine Edwards. Or Rajesh Patel or, if you're a bit younger, Alfie Jackson. Admit it: one of those is your name, isn't it?

I do know a couple of people who have changed their name. An old school friend of mine was genuinely called James Buggerson. I think we can all respect his right to change *his* name. He is now called Alan Buggerson.

After many hours of what-should-we-change-our-name-to conversations in the pub, I have pretty much narrowed down the options. If you are a man it is acceptable to change your name to any of the following:

EDUARDO GONZALEZ

JACK MCMICHAELSON

VANCE CARLISLE

BAN KI-MOON

CARLOS VALENTINO-JONES

JOCK ROCK

MORRISON DANGERWEATHER

BIG EDDIE

If you are a woman you can choose between:

ROXY FOXELBERGER

M'JAZZ LABELLE

RACHEL BENSUAREZ-GOLDFRAPP

MILLICENT NOSTROMO

CONSUELA SMITH-WESTINGHOUSE

COOL SUE

SVETLANA EDWARDS

ELECTROSMASH 3000

Of course, name changing is already a reality for many
women. They never admit it but everyone knows that, after

good looks and a sense of humour, an acceptable surname is high on the list of attributes in a potential husband. Which is why Jack McMichaelson is married and Alan Buggerson is single.

All of which leads us to some *Pointless* questions. The following are all titles of books followed by the real name of their authors. But what did each author change their name to for the publication of the book?

Can you beat your family? Good luck against Uncle Morrison Dangerweather.

## POINTLESS QUIZ

1. A Series of Unfortunate Events (Daniel Handler)
2. A Clergyman's Daughter (Eric Blair)
3. A Clockwork Orange (John Wilson)
4. Heart of Darkness (Józef Teodor Korzeniowski)
5. All Creatures Great and Small (James Alfred Wight)
6. The Seven Crystal Balls (Georges Remi)
7. A Fatal Inversion (Barbara Vine)
8. Smiley's People (David Cornwell)
9. The Adventures of Tom Sawyer (Samuel Clemens)
10. The Lorax (Theodore Geisel)
11. The Running Man (Stephen King)
12. Candide (François-Marie Arouet)
13. Absent in the Spring (Agatha Christie)
14. Through the Looking Glass (Charles Dodgson)

# 58

## ANT OR DEC?

The minute a team becomes successful, whether it's a girl-band, an emerging political party, or an all-dog street-dance ensemble, it is our duty as interested members of the public to try to truffle out their weakness. Why do we do it? Who knows? But somewhere it's encoded in our DNA* that we can't see anything shiny without wanting to kick its tyres. Why do bands split up seemingly at the top of their game? Because hand in hand with their success comes our unequivocal verdict on who in the band we all like, and who we all consider to be the fat, the ugly, or the useless one. A kind of musical version of *Made in Chelsea*, it's as cruel as it's inevitable. Add to that the other stresses of living at close quarters with a group of young adults in their first flush of wealth, influence

...............................................................................

* DNA is a case in point. Double-helix heroes James Watson and Francis Crick were often criticised for their poorly choreographed dance moves and failure to produce that 'difficult' second discovery.

and, in certain cases, even cocaine, and you can see how quickly life could become intolerable.

The teams that last and last, though, are the teams in which the individuals are reconciled to – even happy with – the unequal apportioning of talent and adulation within the unit. In our *Pointless* double act, for example, I recognised long ago that Richard, with his slow wits, terrible people skills and all-round lack of knowledge, was going to be a dead weight in the slipstream of my bravura repartee and razor-sharp back-and-forth ('And what do you get up to in your *spare* time?' Kerpow!), but I have learned to celebrate that. Heck! People *like* the big guy, and so, despite his extravagant trouser allowance, he stays.

But then once every five thousand years along comes a phenomenon so solid that it's unassailable from any side. British entertainment hasn't seen a double act as exquisitely balanced, as matched talent for talent at the very top of the scale, as Ant and Dec since the early Bronze Age, when camp-fire audiences sat enthralled by the lovable antics of Thog and Nicholas Parsons. Ant and Dec are as symmetrical and as satisfying as a rhyming quatrain, proud Geordies, but not too proud (and not too Geordie . . .). They cover each other's straight-man roles, then swoop in like swallows to drop the killer punch-lines. People say, 'I don't know which is Ant and which is Dec,' as if it's a criticism, but that is to miss the point. They are 'One', TV's Holy Trinity,

Ant . . . and . . . Dec.** They are sophisticated, humble, warm, cool, assured, self-deprecating and, best of all, they are a perfect social litmus: if anyone ever wrinkles their nose at Ant and Dec they are generously letting you know that they are an idiot.

To the question 'Ant or Dec?' there is only one answer: 'Ant *and* Dec.'

---

** Even their middle name is DNA backwards. Ant AND Dec contain the building blocks of life itself.

# 57
# HOW MANY PRINGLES SHOULD YOU EAT AT ONCE?

The United Nations Conference on Narcotic and Substance Abuse, which convened in Atlanta in early October 2012, was a four-day convention covering the current major issues and concerns in the world of addictive behaviour. Among subjects discussed were 'The Effect of US Military Action on Afghan Heroin Production', 'International Enforcement Responses to the Unprecedented Rise of Mexican Cocaine Cartels' and 'MDMA? OMG!'

Below is a direct quote from the keynote speech of the conference given by Professor Lars Bergström of the University of Copenhagen.

We have, over the years at these conferences, discussed many new and troubling narcotic phenomena. Some, such as Synthetic Morphamphetamine, have proved to be a mere flash in the pan. Others, such as the rise of crystal meth, troubled us then, and trouble us still more now. But, Conference, I believe one substance above all to be the single most addictive substance on planet Earth. I'm talking, of course, about Pringles. Having studied them for nearly two decades, I am strongly of the opinion that once you pop, it is fair to say that it is demonstrably difficult to stop.

Now, this is a direct quote from a very senior scientist (don't bother Googling it, though. Who has time for that?). But it is not one that will surprise any of us. If you are reading this at Christmas it is almost certain that you are currently near comatose due to over-consumption of salt and vinegar Pringles.

So, if we all love Pringles then where's the argument?

I know exactly what you're saying: 'I've paid good money for this book (well, my son-in-law bought it for me because I once had *Pointless* on when he came to visit, and ever since then he has been convinced that it's my favourite programme, whereas, in all honesty, I'm more of an *Eggheads* fan) and I'm expecting to hear arguments, not some half-formed nonsense about Pringles, backed up by some spurious quote from a conference which I'm not convinced is actually true. In fact – in fact I'm going to Google it right n—'

Whoa there! No need for that. Here's our argument. How many Pringles should you eat in one go?

My children, normally reluctant to help with this book, very kindly helped me to solve this argument. You can try it yourself, if you're near a tube of Pringles. Which, let's face it, you are.

Try eating just the one. Note the texture, the crunch, what food scientists call the 'mouth-feel'. Now mark that experience out of ten.

Now eat two together. Is the flavour more intense? Is the crunch more satisfying? Is the 'mouth-feel' comforting? Once again, note down your marks out of ten.

OK, three now. And remember: this is science, not over-indulgence. In fact, you might want to use a clipboard to write your scores on. That should fool everyone.

You know what comes next: I need you to try four at once. Is this becoming unwieldy, or are you still in your comfort zone?

If you feel you have already passed the optimum amount of Pringles then please put your pen down. I will point out that my son, who is many things but not a fool, kept going all the way up to seven in one go, despite appearing to be in some distress.

Please now add up your marks, then average them out, and you will find you have almost certainly reached the same conclusion as the Osman Pringle Symposium of 2013.

How many Pringles should you eat in one go?

THREE.

# 56

# WHAT IS THE BEST LENGTH FOR A POP SONG?

Pop songs are three minutes long. That's the rule. Make one any longer than that and the ghost of John Peel will be breaking wind in your kitchen before you can say 'Daddio'. Why three minutes? Think about it: 180 seconds . . . the same number as there are degrees in a semi-circle. So, with an A and B side, that's a perfect circle. Which a record is. Tell me that doesn't make sense. Oh, and another thing: three minutes was as much sound as could be crammed onto an old ten-inch 78 r.p.m. disc and so – for practical reasons – the benchmark was set. If that strikes you as the tail wagging the dog, don't worry: the dog bit back. The story goes that the storage capacity of a CD was determined by the owner of Sony demanding that this new-fangled disc be able to contain the whole of Beethoven's 9th Symphony. Or was it ABBA's *Gold*? Whatever, the point's the same.

But even in the days of the 45 r.p.m. and beyond when a single could be as long as anyone could be bothered to make it, the three-minute rule still held. Of course, songs like Radiohead's 'Paranoid Android' (six minutes, twenty-three seconds), Queen's 'Bohemian Rhapsody' (five minutes, fifty-five seconds) and the Stone Roses' 'Fool's Gold' (just under a fortnight) have proven you can still chart with a longer song, but the average length of a successful single remains three minutes. That is why the likes of Mahler, Tchaikovsky and Wagner drove the execs at their record label spare: 'Gustav, Peter, Dick, get it down to three minutes and *then* you'll have a hit. *Then* you'll break away from the stuffed-shirt brigade and be greeted by screaming girls wherever you go. Or, yes, Peter. Boys, if you prefer.'

So, three minutes it is.

Below are fourteen songs all of which came in at two and a half-minutes long or less; the year of their release is in brackets. Can you name the band or artist who had a hit with each?

## POINTLESS QUIZ

1. 'Metal Guru' (1972)
2. 'Some Kinda Earthquake' (1959)
3. 'The Simpsons Theme' (2007)
4. 'All Shook Up' (1957)
5. 'Mr Tambourine Man' (1965)
6. 'Girlfriend In A Coma' (1987)

7. 'Song 2' (1997)
8. 'Not Fade Away' (1964)
9. 'Fell In Love With A Girl' (2002)
10. 'White Riot' (1977)
11. 'I Get Around' (1964)
12. 'Please Please Me' (1963)
13. 'Stay' (1961)
14. 'The Ladies' Bras' (2007)

## POINTLESS FACTS

The shortest UK Top Forty chart-topper is Adam Faith's 'What Do You Want' from 1959 (1 minute, 38 seconds).

'You Suffer' is a song by the British grindcore band *Napalm Death*, from their début album, *Scum*. It earned a place in the *Guinness Book of Records* as the shortest recorded song ever. It is precisely 1.316 seconds long.

# 55

# DID MAN REALLY LAND ON THE MOON?

The world is full of conspiracy theories. Or *is* it? Yes, yes, it is.

We love to believe in elaborate plots designed by shady élites to pull the wool over the eyes of the population for various nefarious purposes.

With this in mind, we turn to *Pointless* viewer Steve Murray, who sent us the following email:

*I have one long-standing argument with my dad and would be grateful if you could investigate.*

*He was born in January 1944 and so was 25 years old when the pinnacle of human achievement was reached and man landed on the moon for the first time. I can imagine the sheer excitement that must have permeated across the*

*world as the seemingly impossible was accomplished.*
*Widespread joy and optimism about what the future could*
*hold must have been almost tangible.*

*As I was born in 1970, I didn't get to experience watching*
*one of the greatest events of my, or any other, lifetime and*
*I have to admit to a certain jealousy of those who were*
*around at the time.*

*It therefore surprises me that my dad is now utterly*
*convinced that the Americans did not land on the moon at*
*all in July 1969 and believes the whole event to have been*
*a charade designed to help the USA avoid Cold War igno-*
*miny. He may have watched Capricorn One a few too many*
*times but, nevertheless, he is immovable in his belief. I, on*
*the other hand, can see no reason to doubt the event*
*happened as reported. But with each new conspiracy*
*theory, his views harden and I struggle to find ways to*
*convince him.*

*So, I implore you, please could you solve this argument: did*
*man really land on the moon in 1969?*

Well, Steve, and, more importantly, Steve's dad, I tend to be
dubious of all conspiracy theories for two major reasons.

1. I have worked in all sorts of companies for many
   years: the idea of a group of people all agreeing on *the*

*same conspiracy*, and then each and every one of them managing not to mess it up, is remote, to say the least. Think about how many scientists, and engineers, and astronauts, and astronaut catering staff there were. Most of whom you can be sure will have hated each other. Then think how hard it is just to organise a *whip-round* at work. Imagine how much harder it would be to *fake a moon landing*, without someone saying, 'We can't do it on Monday because I'm on a half-day and I booked it ages ago.'

And, of course, say that, by some miracle, no one *does* mess it up and the conspiracy succeeds. What are the odds that no one then wants to take the credit? Like Dave from Accounts when your payroll services were all transferred online without a hitch: he couldn't stop crowing about it, could he? Even though it was mainly down to Helen in IT. I'm certain that if NASA *had* conspired to fake the moon landings in 1969, their version of Dave from Accounts would be in his local bar in minutes, saying, 'Yeah, all my idea, actually. A lot of the bosses said it couldn't be faked but, hey, I'm Dave from Accounts and I get stuff done.'

2. The world is indeed being run by powerful shady élites, but they long ago gave up trying to keep anything *secret* from us. Over the last ten years we've been dragged into a crippling recession by a wealthy élite who lost billions upon billions of dollars and

plunged whole countries into crippling poverty. And they haven't needed to keep it secret *at all*. They've just done it and carried on picking up enormous bonuses. And they've also made billions selling arms to blow up countries and then made more billions winning contracts to rebuild the countries that they just bombed. And they do all this on the record and it seems to be OK. I don't know exactly how they do these things, but they do.

The Moon Landings were an example of everything that is best about human endeavour. If you read any contemporary accounts of this extraordinary project your mind simply boggles at the combination of boundless intelligence and peerless bravery that went into one of the most spectacular, if ultimately fairly pointless, achievements in human history.

It *seems* impossible that man went to the moon, using just the computing power equivalent of a digital watch. But they did. If they didn't, there would be enough people with proof and a grudge and a gambling habit that needed funding who would let us know otherwise.

History tells us again and again that the only thing that really, truly endures is the truth. Lies break.

I suppose my conclusion is that, however impossibly difficult it was to put man on the moon, it was nothing compared to how difficult it would be to lie about putting a man on the moon.

Sorry, Steve's dad, but it could be worse. Imagine if Steve ever finally found out about the infamous Pet Goldfish Replacement Conspiracy you and your wife organised when he was six.

## POINTLESS FACTS

During *Apollo* 11's lunar landing, Neil Armstrong had to fly the lunar module manually over West Crater and portions of a boulder field to locate a safe landing site – apparently there was thirty seconds of fuel left at touch-down.

Sergei Krikalyov has spent 803 days, 9 hours and 39 minutes, or 2.2 years, in space over the span of six spaceflights on *Soyuz*, the *Space Shuttle*, *Mir*, and the *International Space Station*. That makes him the spaciest human being ever. Neil Armstrong spent 8 days, 13 hours, 59 minutes in space.

# 54

## SHOULD I TAKE VITAMINS?

It's always nice to be able to blame something. Not necessarily because we want to be vindictive – although that, too, can be fun – but because when things go wrong we need to believe that under normal circumstances things would have turned out so very much better. A disappointing summer? It's the jet stream, my friend. A disappointing result? Why, yes, because the ref might as well have worn your opponents' colours. A disappointing circus? Well, that's what you get when they tighten up animal cruelty laws. Were the dice to have been thrown any differently, everything would be much, much better. Life is, more often than not, a crap-shoot, with the emphasis on crap.

And it's the same with our health, mentally and physically. When we're feeling below par but we know that, strictly speaking, there is nothing *wrong* with us, we have to have somewhere to turn. And what we turn to is vitamins, because we've read about them on the sides of cereal packets. Although we don't understand science, we know the alphabet so we think we have some insight into the difference between Vitamin A, Vitamin B and Vitamin C (which, of course, is in oranges!) so they make us feel not only terrific about ourselves, but also just a little bit brainy. But what are these wonderful life-enhancers? And what makes them so different from life's other enhancements, like kedgeree, say, or vajazzles?

Well, most of the chemicals that our bodies require can be synthesised by our organs,* and so are pretty much taken care of 'in house', but just for fun and to encourage us to get out more (quite literally, as sunshine's packed with Vitamin D), the body requires tiny doses of certain compounds that can only be sourced through consumption of various nutri-ents. And these are our so-called vitamins. We need them in regular but minuscule quantities and, happily, they're present in pretty much everything we like eating or drinking, such as beer and chips – don't let anyone tell you they're bad for you. Somehow, though, when we're feeling put upon, hung-over, stressed, tired or unmotivated, we like to think that sluicing several thousand per cent of our weekly requirement of these compounds in one unreasonably priced effervescent tablet will do wonders for us.

........................................................................................

* This doesn't include alcohol or other recreational substances. Still, who knows what they'll be able to do in a few years? The liver that brews its own booze? This is what science is for.

And to a point they do precisely that because they make us feel like we've taken action. We've assessed what was wrong, worked out that it was probably because we haven't been taking vitamins, and we have taken them. We are both doctor and patient, cunning and stupid, prescribing ourselves placebos that actually do the trick. Is this healthy? Probably not.

So, should you take vitamins? No, you shouldn't. Unless you find yourself at sea for forty days with nothing but ship's biscuit, weevils and a massive jar of MultiVits in which case, yes, you should.

But don't expect to live any longer.

# 53

# IS IT EVER ACCEPTABLE TO DUMP SOMEONE BY TEXT MESSAGE?

How to dump someone is an age-old problem.

If I were writing this in 1985, I'd be asking, 'Is it ever acceptable to dump someone by fax?'

If I were writing this in 1948, I'd be asking, 'Is it ever acceptable to dump someone by carrier pigeon?'

If I were writing this in 15,000 BC I'd be asking 'Is it ever acceptable to dump someone by cave painting?'

Being dumped is dreadful, that's an absolute given. In the relationship algebra of 'It's not you, it's me' it's *always* worse to be the 'you'.

But let's concentrate on the times where we are the dumper, not the dumpee. When it's not them, it's us. Where you just think maybe you want different things, or are travelling in different directions, or are just deliberately moving to Sydney.

We all know that dumping someone face to face is awful. They either know you're going to do it, in which case it's mesmerisingly painful, or they don't know you're going to do it, in which case it's thirty times worse.

We all have that one conversation with our closest confidante where we say, 'But surely it's best for us both if I just send a text, and we won't have to start crying in Pizza Express.' And our closest confidante will always tell us to do it face to face. And that's because:

(a) Our closest confidante is a kind and thoughtful human being.
(b) It's exactly what we told *her* two months ago when she asked if she could dump Ryan by text.

We know we have to dump someone face to face. We understand that that is the most respectful and humane way to do something deeply unpleasant and unwelcome.

So it's never acceptable to dump someone by text message, right?

Wrong. Just hear me out.

I'm assuming that you or I would never dump anyone by text. As you're a fan of *Pointless*, I'm going to guess that you have a thoughtful soul and an empathetic nature. If you didn't, then surely you'd be watching *Tipping Point*.

So, if anyone with a decent bone in their body would never dump you by text, we can deduce that the opposite is also true. Anyone who dumps you by text is an awful, unkind and desperately immature human being.

Thus if you've ever been dumped by text, the heartache is just as keen and raw, but at least you know for a fact that you've been dumped by an *absolute idiot*, and that you've had a very lucky escape.

So, sometimes it is acceptable to dump someone by text. By all means do it if you think it's OK. Because in the long-term it's always nice to have proof that you've been dumped by an imbecile, rather than by a kind, thoughtful, rounded human being.

Which is why somewhere in a French cave seventeen thousand years ago there's a woman looking at a painting of a man chopping up a heart with an axe, and through her tears you can see the beginnings of a smile.

# 52

# ARE OLIVES REVOLTING?

I hope the table below is helpful:

| Olive Colour | Are They Revolting? |
| --- | --- |
| BLACK | YES |
| GREEN | ALMOST ALWAYS |
| GREEN WITH RED BIT INSIDE | MUCH LIKE THE GREEN ONES, BASICALLY |

# IS *THE ONLY WAY IS ESSEX* THE END OF WESTERN CIVILISATION AS WE KNOW IT?

There is a school of thought that programmes such as *The Only Way Is Essex* represent some sort of low point in the cultural history of the planet.

This semi-scripted semi-documentary, following a largely orange cast of characters as they break up, make up and fake up, first hit our screens in 2010 and has spawned countless imitators from *Made In Chelsea* (posh and orange) to *The Valleys* (Welsh and orange) to *Desperate Scousewives* (Liverpudlian, married and orange).

On Twitter I often stick up for television like *TOWIE* and am always met with a torrent of abuse. Apparently it's TV watched by morons, made by morons and starring morons.

Well, let's take those one by one.

*Made by morons.* Definitely not. This type of show tends to be made by very talented people who love what they're doing. They understand their audience in the same way that the makers of *The Culture Show* understand theirs.

*Watched by morons.* Anyone who calls large groups of other people 'morons' because of an entertainment choice is treading the tightrope of irony.

*Starring morons.* OK, by and large, I'll give you that.

It is my view that, in the grand scheme of things, *TOWIE* is an entertainment show on a small channel that appeals to a certain demographic and appeals to them extremely well. It needn't touch your life in any way. The world is full of great art and extraordinary beauty, and there is plenty of room for a little show made with love and a twinkle in its eye.

Of course my defence of *The Only Way Is Essex* has nothing to do with the fact that I was born in Essex myself. And, in celebration, here is a list of clues to some famous folk born in the beautiful county of Essex.

They are not all orange.

# POINTLESS QUIZ

1. Appointed home secretary in 1997.
2. He became *X Factor* presenter in 2007.
3. Presenter of *Deal or No Deal*.
4. Played the title character in *The Prime of Miss Jean Brodie* in 1969.
5. Played the android Ash in *Alien*.
6. Hurdler who won Olympic gold in 1992.
7. *Big Breakfast* presenter who married Lee Mead.
8. Author of *Rivals* and *Riders*.
9. Married Katy Perry in 2010.
10. Wrote controversial play *Blasted*.
11. She appeared in twenty-four *Carry On* films.
12. Derek to Peter Cook's Clive.

# 50

## LOO ROLL – FRONT OR BACK?

Now that the debate over Margaret Thatcher's impact on British life has at long last been decided,* it seems *everyone* is arguing over whether the loo roll should hang down to the front or the back. And yet I'm baffled: where's the argument? There is only one correct answer. Of the ten random people I asked, all ten said the same thing: to the front, you weirdo, now will you kindly get out of my house – and, no, you can't use it on the way out. When asked why, the reasons were clear (*and* hilarious):

1.  'That way, the sheet of loo roll is nearer to the user.' Who'd have thought it?  Those straining sounds you hear coming from the loo can, more often than not, be attributed to the user stretching an arm that extra ten centimetres out of the shoulder socket to reach the sheet.

..................................................................................................

*Opponents have agreed to disagree.

2. 'The outside of the roll (yes, apparently they have an outside) is presented to the user and hides the workings behind it.' This is possibly the most unimpressive use of the word 'workings' I have ever heard. What is hidden? More loo roll. Which is surely a reassuring sight.

3. 'So the loo roll isn't hanging down against the wall: that way you don't have to reach underhand and pull.' Another anti-straining argument, with the added insinuation that a potentially germ-laden wall is not something you want in contact with the paper, which is about to come in contact with your bum.

And, best of all,

4. 'Because that's how professionals do it in hotels when they fold it into a neat V.' This does, of course, assume that the professionals who prepare your bathroom have your best interests at heart. But why should a cleaner on the minimum wage have any time for the moneyed ponces who mess up the beds, undo all the tidying and make the towels far wetter than they would if they were at home? What if the professionals know the 'best way' is to hang it at the back and, for them, to do the opposite is one of the only pleasures of their working day? That, and adding a cleverly coded V sign.

However, it's hard to argue with the following:

5. Is there anything else we pull off a roll (Sellotape, kitchen towel, tin foil, clingfilm) that we would consider – even for a moment – pulling from the far side? Of course not.

It's a pure, logical argument that has not been bettered since first used by Aristotle while queuing by a cesspit in Athens.**

But still we have not learned. I suspect the argument that simmers in every bathroom from Truro to Tillicoultry goes something like this:

**A**

Who put the loo roll in?

**B**

Uh?

**A**

Did you put the loo roll in? It must've been you because it's in the wrong way.

**B**

Wha'?

**A**

It's in the wrong way. It should hang down to the front.

**B**

Oh.

........................................................................................................

** Loo roll was a contentious issue among the philosophers of Ancient Greece, except of course for the Stoics, who just used their hands.

In seven out of ten times B is a male. And in ten out of ten times, he'd actually been quite pleased with himself for the skill with which he'd performed the re-stocking . . . but that glow of satisfaction is now a distant memory.

In cases where people have a preference it is unanimously for the hanging sheet to come forwards. But the issue is, should we really be bothered about this? Shouldn't we just settle for being glad that we've even got some loo roll, that someone remembered to change it*** and, for heaven's sake, that we no longer use a stone, or that greaseproof stuff that, just like Classix Nouveaux, found its timely extinction some time in the eighties?

I am genuinely pleased when loo roll hangs down to the back – because it is evidence that whoever put it in doesn't give a crap about which way it should go, and that has got to be healthy. So . . .

Should the loo roll hang to the front? Yes, apparently it should. Should we care about which way it hangs? Really no.

.............................................................................

*** If your answer to this is 'What's the big deal?', then you have never sat in a public cubicle, dismantling a cylinder of curled cardboard, in a vain effort to create a usable surface.

# 49
# SHOULD YOU TAKE A PACKED LUNCH TO WORK?

In an office, lunch can prove to be quite an event. A chance to pop out of a stale, fluorescently lit building and take in the bracing air of a Braintree winter. Then the choice – the glorious choice! What will it be today? Morrisons? Greggs? Wait! The Mighty Bap has just reopened after that health-and-safety scare! Then skipping gleefully back to HQ to eat at speed, dropping crumbs that will never escape those weird crevices in your computer keyboard, before a fun afternoon of explaining to Jonathan from Sales why Laser Quest doesn't count as a legitimate business expense.

But not everybody has these twenty-seven minutes of joy in their day – and you know exactly who I'm talking about. The people who bring a packed lunch into work. Them. A sandwich, a little pot of couscous and a piece of fruit. They have three arguments in their favour. Let's take these one by one.

1. *Having a packed lunch saves time.* Definitely true, but hold on. The whole point of work is that you don't *want* to save time. You want to *waste* time. A packed lunch absolutely gets in the way of this. Don't forget that the trip to Morrisons also works as an opportunity to get away from your phone, your emails, your supervisor Janet and, if you time it just right, you might also miss the whip-round for Carl's leaving present. It's also a chance to check out those four guys doing their Community Service, dredging the canal with their tops off. I think the one with the spider's web tattoo on his face might be single.

2. *Having a packed lunch saves money.* You've saved about £1.70 by making your lunch at home, but you've just put in £2 for Carl's present. And you *hate* Carl.

3. *A packed lunch is healthier.* Nonsense, I'm afraid. Due to advances in the science of food-combining, nutritionists have recently revealed that the healthiest possible lunch is actually a sandwich, a packet of Quavers, a bottle of Lucozade and a bag of Cadbury's Mini Eggs.

So, no, you should not take a packed lunch into work. And if you *do*, it should act only as a 'secondary' lunch you can eat at about three-ish because, for some reason, that packet of Quavers hasn't quite filled you up.

# 48

# IS THIS MAN-FLU THING ACTUALLY A BIT TIRESOME?

Man-flu. Forgive me while I laugh.* So where did this man-flu business come from? My guess is that it germinated – like so many of these things do – in someone's clever stand-up routine probably some time around 2004. The man-flu gag will then have migrated up to Edinburgh for the fringe festival in August of that year where it will have sat gestating in the near-perfect incubation conditions of one of the smaller and sweatier Pleasance venues. Here it will have landed on several receptive surfaces during the three-week run and thereby been dispersed around the country. Back in London, as the laughter became more infectious, one strain of the gag will have gradually mutated, jumping for the first time from the original comedian's set list onto those of other, less hard-working,

..........................................................................................

* A-ha-ha-ha-ha-haaaaa. A-ha ha-ha-ha, a-ha, a-ha, a-ha-ha-ha-ha-haaaaaaa. Oh, God, a-ha, ha, oh that's excellent. Man-flu! Ha! Oh dear, no, I'm fine.

stand-ups, known in the business as 'carriers' or 'plagiarising bastards'. Then some time in the early spring of 2005 the DNA will have mutated again, jumping this time from lacklustre open spots around the capital to the printed page, appearing first in an op-ed column on London's *Evening Standard* and then, in June, in the 'What's Hot, What's Not' barometer of the *Sunday Times* Style section and officially reaching 'epidemic' level. From which point an unaggressive variant of the gag will have entered everyday parlance where it will have lain dormant for three and a half years before eventually entering the bloodstream of advertising, a body of so-called creatives with zero resistance to nicking other people's old ideas. That is – at the very least – a plausible genesis for the expression.**

But is there any substance to it? Is it true that men are terrible hypochondriacs? Did Achilles actually whinge about his heel? Whatever pain George V was feeling on his deathbed, he still chose to go out with the words 'Bugger Bognor'. And even a wuss like Oscar Wilde chose to discuss wallpaper when he snuffed it rather than bang on about his earache. In fact, there has been extensive polling and adding up of statistics and, although there is no actual data on levels of melodramatic behaviour among men with minor ailments, in the two surveys I could be bothered to look up

** It is also the longest extended metaphor I have ever attempted. Feel a bit woozy, actually . . .

online,*** the average man seems to take 2.8 days off a year through illness compared to the average woman taking off three. So unless, of course, women are being really brave and should actually be taking thirty days off, it is possible that men are being maligned by this man-flu jibe.

The truth is, though – as anyone who has answered the phone to a person calling in sick will attest – few things are more irritating than someone exaggerating an illness, partly because you have no choice but to join their pathetic conspiracy. What's more, this croaky pulling of a sickie is never going to sound more ridiculous than when it's coming from someone who spends the rest of the time trying to be the big alpha male. So, taking that into account, along with my desperate wish to come across as a man who is big enough to laugh at himself, I say that the Man-flu Thing, far from being tiresome, is in fact really very funny.**** Carry on with your man-flu jokes. Now, if you'll excuse me, I need a lie-down.

........................................................................................

*** Yes: note that's not *one* source but *two*, i.e. proper journalistic practice (even though I'm pretty sure one website had just copied the other).
**** See *.

# POINTLESS FACTS

The word 'influenza' comes from the Italian 'influential' because people used to believe that the influence of the planets, stars and moon caused flu, for only such universal influence could explain such sudden and widespread sickness.

The 1918 flu pandemic infected 500 million people across the world, including remote Pacific islands and the Arctic, and killed up to 100 million of them – three to five per cent of the world's population at the time. The total number of military and civilian casualties in the First World War was about 37 million. The Spanish flu killed more Americans in one year than the combined total who died in battle during the First World War, the Second World War, the Korean War and the Vietnam War.

# 47

# DO I HAVE TO CALL LORD SUGAR 'LORD SUGAR'?

When we asked *Pointless* viewers to send us their arguments for this book we had lots of lovely emails. We also had lots of, frankly, disturbing emails and, rest assured, we have alerted the relevant authorities. In other email news, we won't have to write another *Pointless* book next year because I have won the Nigerian lottery. But I digress.

Bernadette emailed us to say: 'My boyfriend says if he met Lord Sugar, he would call him Mr Sugar, or Alan, but I think that would be rude.'

Hmm, I know what he means. Just because the Queen or someone decides that Alan Sugar is a lord, it doesn't mean I necessarily agree. But, in general, you should probably call people what they want to be called. That is the polite thing to do, though by all means slag them off in the car on the way home.

Whenever I order things online and fill in my name I try to pick different titles, so I often get letters for Professor Richard Osman, Rev. Richard Osman and Mrs Richard Osman. It really brightens up my mornings. You should try it.

Below is another of our *Pointless* quizzes. This is what they call in publishing 'added value'. Good, eh?

You're going to see a list of different awards and honours, and you just have to say in which country each is awarded. My tip for this quiz is to bet your dad £1,000 that he can't guess 'Order of the Elephant' in five goes.

## POINTLESS QUIZ

1. Order of the White Lion
2. Order of Isabella the Catholic
3. Order of the Elephant
4. Order of the House of Orange
5. Order of the Nile
6. Presidential Medal of Freedom
7. Legion of Honour
8. Order of the Rising Sun
9. Order of the Aztec Eagle
10. Silver Laurel Leaf
11. Order of the Seraphim
12. Padma Vibhushan

# 46

## SHOULD I TELL SOMEONE WHAT THEY REALLY LOOK LIKE IN THEIR TROUSERS?

If anyone asks you what you think of their trousers, they are not interested in what you think of their trousers. This may seem paradoxical, but that's because it's a paradox. It dates back to Ancient Greece, when the philosopher Zeno of Elea was first asked by his boyfriend what he thought of his new skirt, a question that had far more ramifications than the one Zeno was working on at the time, which was whether Achilles could outrun a tortoise.* If anyone asks you what you think of their trousers, they don't want to know if you like the cut, they do not want your opinion on the colour, they mean – literally – can I get away with these with my arse? That's what 'What do you think of these jeans?' means. (And if anyone ever asks you, 'Can I get away with these with my arse?' there is only one answer you can give, and

..........................................................................................

* The answer to that one is 'yes': 100 metres, 400 metres, 1,500 metres, marathon, whatever. Tortoises simply lack the will to win.

it's 'Totally!' The good thing about this latter scenario is that you are 100 per cent safe. If they're the ones that brought up the whole arse thing, they clearly know it's an issue. They will also know that you have lied, but for the sweetest of motives. It's a law that's been around longer than habeas corpus.** When anyone asks a direct question about their arse, the truth is simply not on the agenda. Unless, of course, you're a proctologist.)

When you are presented with a pair of trousers to appraise, they will be walked towards you – or, if they're *really* tight, squeegeed – and then the wearer will stagily strike a pose that will be somewhere between what they consider to be a normal way of standing and what they consider to be rather a fetching posture for them. Your job is ALWAYS to greet their appearance with your head slightly to one side, your hands out in front of you as if you are presenting a ten–twelve-pound salmon to them and say the words, 'Oh! Those are amazing! You look incredible.'

There are some people to whom you owe the courtesy of candour (a sibling, say, or spouse), someone who will remember that you said the trousers were fine when they are later studying photographs of themselves signally *not* getting away with those trousers with their arse. In which

..............................................................................

** Which, coincidentally, is Latin for 'You have the body' (to get away with those trousers).

case don't panic: the rules are very simple. You just need to wolf whistle, shake your hand like you've burned it on something and say, 'Bloody *hell* they look incredible on you,' and, after a brief moment, add, 'They're very blue those ones, though, aren't they? Maybe a bit *B\*Witched*? Actually, it's not the blue so much, it's the stitching.' Anyway, you get the idea.

Do we ever, ever tell people what they really look like in their trousers? Absolutely not.

# 45

# WHAT IS THE BEST AND WORST SWEET IN THE VARIOUS LARGE TINS OF CHOCOLATES WE CURRENTLY HAVE ON THE SIDEBOARD?

Most of the things we now associate with a traditional Christmas were first introduced in Victorian times. In fact, our modern Christmas owes more to *A Christmas Carol* by Charles Dickens than to the Bible by God.

But one utterly central Christmas tradition is even more recent. Absolutely enormous tins of sweets!

The key dates in the history of absolutely enormous tins of sweets are as follows:

*1936*: Quality Street are introduced by Mackintosh. John Mackintosh had opened the world's first toffee factory in Halifax in 1898. It burned down in 1908, which must have smelt delicious. John's son, Harold, introduced Quality Street as the first low-cost chocolate assortment, and he named them after a J. M. Barrie play, which you would think was a weird thing to name chocolates after, until you get to . . .

*1938*: Roses are introduced by Cadburys. Now, *they* were named after Rose Brothers, the English *packaging-equipment company* that provided the machinery to wrap the sweets. I don't think they had branding agencies back then.

*1939–96*: fifty-seven years pass by. Nothing much happens in the world, until . . .

*1997*: Mars brings out Celebrations, which were named after, um, things people do when they celebrate. They probably paid someone hundreds of thousands of pounds to think that up, and it doesn't seem a whole lot better than Roses. Though I have no accurate information about the packaging-equipment company that provides the machinery to wrap the sweets. I'm guessing they're Korean?

*1999*: Miniature Heroes are born. Cadburys follow their now traditional path of letting another company bring out an enormous tin of sweets, watching it for two years to see if it makes any money, then copying it. Miniature Heroes were named in honour of a gang of chocolate scientists who were tragically shrunk in an industrial accident.

And, of course, 'What's the best sweet in the tin?' and 'What's

the worst sweet in the tin?' are now two of the most common
Christmas arguments, behind only 'How are you supposed
to get this battery compartment open?' and 'Is Uncle Keith
sleeping, or has he finally died?'

These arguments are by no means easy (except Celebrations,
which is obvious) but let's get it done. Feel free to treat this
entry as interactive. Tell your mum I said it was OK.

## *QUALITY STREET*

Personally, I like the orange and strawberry creams best, but,
hey, this book isn't all about me (I've just checked the contract.
I'm fuming).

Green triangle? Iconic, but a bit dull. We also have to rule out
the toffees, don't we? Worst of all, of course, the toffee penny.
Which leaves us with coconut éclair (too exotic), vanilla fudge
(too vanilla-y, and too fudgey), caramel swirl (can't even
remember it; caramel swirl is like the drummer out of
Coldplay). And so we are left with one winner. A relative
newcomer to Quality Street. It's citrusy, it's hexagonal, it's the
*orange crunch*.

## *ROSES*

So, again, I have to rule out the two fruit creams. We then
lose the worst sweet in the pack, the Brazilian darkness
(almost as bad as the toffee penny in Quality Street). Fudge
is out, Dairy Milk block shows no imagination. If you like

Dairy Milk, why would you have the tiniest one in the world? That leaves us with the two hazelnut contenders, one in caramel, the other in a swirly chunk of chocolate. And, after a process of elimination (which is how I describe the act of eating), the winner is *hazelnut swirl*.

## CELEBRATIONS

Obviously Maltesers. Best by a mile. Worst Milky Way. Mars is making that one pretty easy for us all. Wow, just imagine if the *Maltesers factory* burned down! That would be some tourist attraction.

## MINIATURE HEROES

Over the years Cadburys have chopped and changed the line-up of Miniature Heroes, to the point at which I think they now have the weakest selection they've ever had. Gone are Bourneville (fair enough), Crunchie (mistake), Fuse (sadly no longer with us), Whole Nut (also fair enough), Flake (big error, but maybe couldn't live alongside Twirl), Picnic (a bit of variety) and Time Out (the single most underrated chocolate bar of them all). So what's left? Dairy Milk (you've already done this one, Cadburys), Fudge (yawn), Caramel, Creme Egg Twisted (I've got quite a sweet tooth, but these are too much even for me). Which leaves us with our best and worst. Worst, clearly Éclair, and best of a bad bunch, *Twirl*.

So, those are the definitive answers. But this is one of those lovely arguments where it pays to be on the losing side. No matter where you go for Christmas, you know that if you're a fan of the toffee penny, Brazilian darkness, Milky Way or Éclair you will always be welcome.

# 44

# ARE FILM REMAKES EVER ANY GOOD?

Every couple of years or so a poster really grabs your attention. Actually, that's not very often at all – so, ironically, not a great advert for adverts. Anyway, the reason this poster grabs your attention is not because you suddenly think, Yes, I *do* have a really good chance of winning the Euromillions lottery this week, even though they couldn't find a winner last week or the week before, a flaw in their system which they seem oddly proud about. Neither does this poster grab your attention because no girl in the world really has breasts like that. No, you walk past a poster, or maybe it drives past you on the side of a bus, and you stop dead and think, What? They've remade *that*? With *HIM*? and a tiny little piece of you falls to the ground, beating its balled and bloody fists into the pavement and screaming, NOOOOOOO! (It's also at this point you realise you've missed your bus.) I imagine you would get a similar feeling if you rounded a corner expecting to see the house you grew up in with the climbing roses just coming into bloom and your beloved dog getting up from his idle testicle-cleansing in the hazy spring sunshine and lolloping forward to lick your face lovingly, but instead you discover that the whole site has been developed into the UK's biggest Dunkin Donuts. And who's this in the foreground? Why it's Eddie Murphy. And he's nailing that dog to the front door.*

Yes, there have been successful remakes over the years but mainly when they're new adaptations of a book. The works of Dickens, Jane Austen, the Brontë sisters, Bram Stoker and Thomas Hardy are being continually remade. It is, in fact, possible for every person in China to watch a different film version of *Dracula* simultaneously. And it's these 1.2 billion different *Dracula*s that are the main reason that Christopher Lee is not as well known in China as his brother Bruce. Why do Hollywood producers love 'book-movies'? Because it's the nearest they get to reading one. 'Heck, that's got a lot of pages. Film it, Ang! *Then* I'll take a look.'

The other 'natural' remake is, of course, when the original film was in a foreign language. 'Ah,' reasons the studio boss. 'This ancient British movie that found worldwide affection in the fifties kinda *is* in a foreign language. If we set it in modern-day America and attach a big-name star** we can

......................................................................................

* You will say if I'm overdoing it?
** From 1985.

tell the story all over again. After all, new versions of plays are being put on every day and what about cover versions of songs, for goodness' sake? If Rolf Harris can cover "Stairway To Heaven", then dammit, we can remake *The African Queen* with Jennifer Aniston.'

'Well, you're right, boss,' says his lickspittle sidekick, as he packs up his desk and decides to go and work with under-privileged children instead. 'It's just every sane person instantly recognises these films as bloodless exercises in craven money-making that insult the industry that once brought so much joy to the world. If you want my opinion,' continues Lickspittle Sidekick, with a new confidence, 'you should be investing money in original films, like that British script, whatsitcalled, the *Pointless* movie?'

But, no, *Step Up To the Podium*, with Hugh Bonneville as an inept and floundering quiz-show host and Denzel Washington as his *Pointless* friend, will never be made. It's a crying shame, because once they'd made it, they'd definitely want to make it again.

Film remakes are never any good. The problem is, they're remaking the wrong films. Where's the sense in remaking films that got it massively right first time around? They should start remaking the films that were terrible and then they might be onto something.

Here are some questions to probe how well you know your film remakes. The following pairs of actors each played the same character in a film. One in the original, one in the remake, and the year of each is shown in brackets. You need to name the film.

## POINTLESS QUIZ

1. Kevin Bacon (1984)
2. Kenny Womad (2011)
3. Audrey Hepburn (1954)
4. Julia Ormond (1995)
5. Fay Wray (1933)
6. Naomi Watts (2005)
7. Frank Sinatra (1960)
8. George Clooney (2001)
9. Arnold Schwarzenegger (1990)
10. Colin Farrell (2012)
11. Noomi Rapace (2009)
12. Rooney Mara (2011)
13. Michael Caine (1966)
14. Jude Law (2004)
15. Steve McQueen (1968)
16. Pierce Brosnan (1999)
17. Katharine Ross (1975)
18. Nicole Kidman (2004)
19. Dudley Moore (1981)
20. Russell Brand (2011)
21. Janet Leigh (1960)

22. Anne Heche (1998)
23. John Wayne (1969)
24. Jeff Bridges (2010)

# IS DARTS BETTER
# THAN OPERA?

Sisters marrying brothers, sons murdering fathers, once-mighty kings losing their thrones to upstart pretenders.

So, that's darts dealt with, but what about opera?

Overweight divas with ridiculous names and outrageous costumes, striding the . . . No, wait, this is still darts. Let's just move on.

You knew that at some point we were going to have to deal with Darts v. Opera, didn't you? Up and down the country, in saloon bars, in open-plan offices, on high-security prison wings, on low-security prison wings, in dog-grooming parlours, and in specialist cheese-packing and distribution depots, this debate has raged for centuries. Here's an absolutely typical argument I overheard the other day in my local library:

**PERSON 1**

Darts is much better than opera!

**PERSON 2**

No way! Opera is much better than darts!

**LIBRARIAN**

Sssh, ladies! This is a library.

**PERSON 1/PERSON 2**

Ooh, sorry.

**PERSON 4**

Hello, I'm afraid I'm a few days late with this John Grisham.

**LIBRARIAN**

That's no problem. Let me just look up the fine for you. That will be . . . one pound seventy, please.

**PERSON 4**

That's gone up, hasn't it?

**LIBRARIAN**

We put the fees up in March, just for inflation and whatnot.

**PERSON 4**

Oh, well, that seems sensible. I thought I might try an Ian Rankin next. Could you recommend a good one?

**LIBRARIAN**

Oh, he's wonderful. If I were you I'd start with one of the early Rebus ones.

**PERSON 4**

Ooh, yes, I've seen a couple of those on ITV.

**PERSON 5** (*standing in queue, beginning to look anxious*)

I'm so sorry, I'm in a bit of a hurry?

**LIBRARIAN**

Sorry! Listen to us yakking away!

**PERSON 5**

Just . . . lunch hour, you know?

**LIBRARIAN**

Working you hard, are they?

**PERSON 5**

Don't they always!

**PERSON 4**

See you, Janice.

**LIBRARIAN**

See you, Lucy!

**PERSON 5**

You don't have the new Marian Keyes, do you?

**LIBRARIAN**

Ooh, yes, and it's very . . .

Let's leave that there.

Now, I accept that the whole conversation isn't relevant, but the stuff at the beginning was pretty powerful, wasn't it?

Let's pose some basic questions about darts and opera and see if one of them begins to edge ahead of the other.

1. Which is more entertaining?
   Darts
2. Which is cheaper?
   Darts
3. At which can you drink more?
   Darts
4. Which one gives its stars nicknames like 'Bravedart' and 'The Prince of Dartness'?
   Opera (check this)
5. In which one do you have to finish on a double?
   Darts (unless it's an opera about some form of mistaken identity, which, actually, almost all operas are, so also Opera)
6. Which one is better?
   Darts

# 42

# ARE THERE TOO MANY FESTIVALS?

How many fields are there in Britain? Shouldn't at least some of them be left to grow some food?

# 41

# SHOULD WE ABOLISH THE ROYAL FAMILY?

We're obsessed with the royals in Britain. Whether they're opening a new leisure centre in Swindon, in hospital with a touch of that bug you had when you got back from Tenerife, or simply minding their own business, buried under a Leicester car park, we can't seem to get enough.

But do we really need them? Are they relevant in 2013 or 2014 or whenever you're reading this book? (And if you're reading this in 2438, then wow, what's *that* like? Is *Bargain Hunt* still going?)

A lot depends on how you word the question. For example, 'Do you like the Queen?' will elicit a very different response from 'Are you happy to pay for Prince Edward's butler?'

I think we all like it when the Queen jumps out of a plane with James Bond, and we like the barely disguised panic in her eyes when she introduces Prince Philip to a visiting African dignitary. We like it when some royal spokesman pretends to apologise for whatever Harry's been up to now, and most women love a nice wedding or baby story (and most men are wise enough to pretend that they do too).

But we're less keen on watching Charles skiing, while we pay £4.70 for a pack of Duchy Original Shortbreads. We also view funding the lifestyle of Prince Andrew in much the same way as we view lending Uncle Keith twenty pounds. We *really* don't want to know what he's going to spend it on, but we know for sure we'll never see it again.

So perhaps we should simply pose the question: what could 52p buy you? A pint of milk? Most of a bag of Quavers? Nearly a first-class stamp? Not much, right?

Well, in 2012, the best 52p you, the taxpayer, spent was to secure another year's access to the never-ending soap opera that is the British Royal Family.

OK, let's clarify a few things first: yes, you didn't have any choice *but* to pay that 52p and, yes, to some people our Royal Family represents an outdated, fusty anachronism that serves no purpose but to give this country an air of superiority and hark back to a bygone era. But 52p! Come on.

From a purely economic standpoint this one is an absolute

no-brainer. Yes, our taxes could be spent on different things – better things some might say, like roads or teachers, but have you ever seen 52p worth of tarmac? It's as boring as hell: 52p worth of tarmac would NEVER play strip billiards in a Las Vegas penthouse or say something vaguely racist to a visiting head of state. It would just lie there, being tarmac.

And give 52p to a teacher and they will all be honest enough to admit that they will simply put it towards a bottle of red wine in their latest desperate attempt to blot out any memory of Michael Gove.

It's not cool to like the Royal Family. I understand that. They're like a national embarrassing relative, never quite getting things right but their heart is squarely in the right place. And, let's be honest, you'd be a little bit sad to see them go.

If you're still unsure, I'll leave you with this poser: if we get rid of the Royal Family, who would you have smash champagne against our yachts, open our hospital wards or pose for our stamps? Piers Morgan?

# 40

## SHOULD I SIT OR HOVER?

This is a thorny one that has occupied senior common rooms and broken up professional-class dinner parties for decades. When Henry Kissinger made his second trip to China in October 1971 the oil in Beijing burned long into the night as the great statesman and his hosts discussed a possible way forward on this issue: whether you should sit on a loo-seat that isn't your own, or whether you should in fact hover above it.* As the hours passed, delegates would at intervals excuse themselves and return a few minutes later to a sea

..................................................................................

* Kissinger was the man for the job. A man of highly visible gut and the kind of gravitas that political commentators sometimes refer to as 'bottom'. A close ally of Richard Nixon during the Watergate scandal, he has confided to historians that the famous 'missing eighteen minutes' of recorded tape was, in fact, full of Nixon cursing and making embarrassing noises in the executive washroom.

of expectant faces, hoping for fresh insight, but a breakthrough remained elusive. An all-night sitting was followed by an all-night hovering, but these talks soon collapsed, along with the delegates. So, alas, no solution was found, and to this day the argument and its attendant bitterness have simmered on, with any debate guaranteed to leave a room divided and in bad odour.

Until now. Since July 2010, Richard Osman and I have been special envoys of the Quartet on Whether to Sit On or to Hover Over Any Loo-seat You Don't Quite Trust based in Vilnius. We have participated in dialogues, summits and conferences the world over, and shortly before writing this volume we were privileged to be signatories to the Treaty of Gdansk,** an historic international agreement that paves the way for a United Nations resolution slated for April 2015, championed by the appropriately named Ban Ki-moon.

I will attempt to précis several long years of discussion by saying the following: it was noted that hand hygiene was considered of paramount desirability to most people. Indeed the committee found that the majority of respondents would even open the door of a loo with their elbows or the little fingers of their left hands to avoid risk of contamination.

...........................................................................................

** A port in Poland. Selected as a venue for its easy accessibility to the numerous plumbers called as expert witnesses.

This raised certain questions*** internationally, not least among the Arab delegates who traditionally use their left hands for unhygienic manual tasks (*and* hygienic ones if they're convicted shoplifters), but was broadly condoned at all levels.

At the next stage of discussion, however, it was pointed out that our backsides were less important, hygienically speaking. As one delegate put it, we were unlikely ever to be eating our breakfast off our (or anyone else's) bottoms. It was recognised that in general there was little to be feared from the communal contact of posterior flesh on a loo-seat as levels of cleanliness in that area were unanimously high. In certain rare circumstances when the loo-seat was demonstrably unclean, there were grounds to wait for a cleaner loo to become available. But the findings of the Quartet were agreed first by a show of hands, and then by a show of bottoms: for heaven's sake, sit.****

......................................................................
*** And sniggers.
**** Although it was noted by the Austrian delegation that hovering is very good for your calves, adductors and glutes.

# 39

# WHO SHOULD BE IN CHARGE OF THE REMOTE CONTROL?

There are very strict rules in Washington about who has access to the 'red button'. That's the button which can ulti-mately launch a nuclear strike and annihilate the world count-less times over.

If a president wishes to launch an attack, he must first issue a coded signal to the joint chiefs of staff, and receive a coded acknowledgement in return. The president must then select a pre-set military plan from the OPLAN 8010 schedule, and communicate this to the National Military Command Centre. The NMCC must positively identify the president using another unique code, and each and every step and decision must then be retaken by the secretary of state for defense under the 'two-man rule'. The process must then be re-verified in full. Then, and only then, can we all go BOOM!

And yet when it comes to the remote control in your living

room there are no such rules or protocols. Even though the consequences of the wrong person gaining control of the remote are far worse than the annihilation of the world. You might, for example, end up having to watch *The Chase*. With this oversight in mind I have drawn up a legally binding set of rules and protocols to govern use, and punish misuse, of the remote control.

The parties undersigned heretowith, and in perpetuity, do, without hindrance or encumbrance, and waiving any and all rights, agree without prejudice, blah blah blah, you're not still reading this bit, are you? That's how lawyers make their money: couple of boring lines up the top to stop you reading, then just any old nonsense. Shopping lists, gobbledegook. Bicycle, eggplant, radiator.

1. No turning off *Call the Midwife* to watch *Live Spanish Football* without full written consent of over 50 per cent of everyone in the living room.
2. That's too loud, turn it down. I don't want John and Pat next door to know we watch *X Factor*.
3. If you have switched over to watch *Top Gear* during the adverts, you must count down the seconds in your head from ninety, and switch over *immediately* you get to zero, even if Jeremy Clarkson is driving a dumper truck into a caravan full of fireworks.
4. When flicking through the channels, you must wait for at least 1.27 seconds on each channel. Don't think that

by skipping through ITV2 at extra speed I'm going to miss the fact that *The Only Way Is Essex – Live!* is on. Nice try, though.

5. When you're fast-forwarding through the adverts, stop trying to show off by going at X32 speed throughout and then overshooting by miles so I have to watch the first thirty seconds of the next part of the show in extreme fast-forward and then extreme reverse as you start to panic. We know the rules. First four adverts at X32, next two at X16, then slow to X8 when they start showing the trailer for that new Martin Clunes thing.

6. When I come in unexpectedly, and you have your finger on the remote, and you're watching *Arabic News*, I know you were watching something you didn't want me to see, so don't try to pretend otherwise ('You know I've always been interested in the Yemen'). I'm hoping you were just watching pornography but, knowing you, it was probably *Pro-Celebrity Ten-pin Bowling* on ESPN2.

Signed:
Witnessed by:
Date:

This document is legally binding, and you should make it a rule in your house that only people who have signed and dated it should be allowed access to the remote control.

I hope this helps.

# 38
## HOW DO WE FEEL ABOUT POSTMAN PAT?

'Pat feels he's a really happy man'. These are the last words we hear at the end of every single episode of *Postman Pat* (trust me, I've seen them all . . . many times). They hang in the air for long, long seconds until the CBeebies continuity announces that *Everything's Rosie* is coming up next.

I think this curiously off-note epitaph deserves a closer look because the words are quite deliberate (they're heard three times throughout the song). The lyricist *could* have written: 'Pat feels he's a really *lucky* man' (or better still 'Pat *knows* he's a really lucky man'), which would sign off the lyric with an elegant flourish and, moreover, would put Pat in the gracious position of acknowledging the affection he's held in and even – to some degree – reciprocating it. This would make Pat, in his special song, a more empathic character within his working community. And if no mention is made of Pat's 'happiness' or otherwise, we could merely note the sentiment of the song ('Birds are singing', 'All his friends will smile as he waves', etc.) and draw the natural conclusion that Pat is indeed happy and leave it at that.

But those are not the words.

Pat feels he's a really happy man. What strange kind of disconnect is going on here? Either Pat is happy or he's not. Something's up. But what? There are two possible explanations. The answer lies either in the mind of the songwriter . . . or in the mind of Pat himself.

To start with, the songwriter. Does he know more than he's letting on? Is he, for all the sunny innocence of the rest of the lyrics, in fact deeply sceptical about the happiness Pat has found? Sure, if you ask Pat, 'Are you truly happy?', Pat will give the entirely honest answer, 'Yes, I am.' But such easy contentment jars with a professional lyricist who, dividing his time between the cutthroat worlds of advertising jingles and children's telly, lives in a far harsher, far cooler urban environment than this simple village postman. Ah, thinks the savvy songster, you, Pat, you, in your ignorance, think you're happy but that is only because you have never travelled more than ten miles out of Greendale. Your horizons are as narrow as a hamster's in its cage, a hamster for which bliss is to run round and round in a wheel and stop for an occasional seed, nut or drink of water from an absurdly designed metal tube. You, Postman Pat, don't know what real human happiness is. You are a happy man? No, no, no, you feel you are a happy man. You, Postman Pat, are as happy as a hamster. Your 'genuine happiness' is genuinely sad. There is such a huge, wide world out there to explore and revel in, but for you it starts and ends with a cardboard backdrop of green hills and blue sky. You think you're happy? OK, don't worry, I'll do nothing to shatter your illusions with this, the Postman Pat song.

And yet . . . and yet my Leonard Cohen side demands that I at least hint at the truth.

Or . . . there is a darker interpretation.

Pat knows.

Pat knows he's not happy. And never will be. Let's face it, who would ever express their state of mind by saying they 'feel they are a happy person' unless they were answering a question in a survey? And in the midst of Pat's enviable work environment and companions (let's not forget that this is a man who takes his black and white cat to work), this strange noncommittal summary invites doubt for what it leaves out. This is the 'whatever love means' of children's television. This Pat needs help. This Pat, after another long day of lugging Amazon boxes in and out of the van, after delivering card after card, saying, 'Sorry you were out, now go to the depot', has finally stopped his van in a layby near a farm and taken

200

a long, hard look at himself, a long, hard look at the man he *could* have become. Paddy, boy, Paddy, whatever happened to those teenage dreams of forming a rock band? When you fantasised about touring the country in a van, did you really think it would be a red one bearing the insignia of Royal Mail? And as for the pussy you pictured yourself with, well . . . Dame Fate cruelly misinterpreted that one. And what about that novel you were going to write? Oh, yes, you're a man of letters, all right!

'I'm happy, Jess, I'm happy, I'm happy!' This is the real Postman Pat, a lonely bachelor, middle-aged before his time, talking to his cat. A few sessions of therapy and we'd soon have you in tears, my four-eyed friend.

Whichever explanation you choose, there can be no doubt: everything is emphatically not rosy with Pat. 'Pat feels he's a very happy man': this is the phrase we'll all be tearing apart for answers when Pat finally goes postal. So, how do we feel about Postman Pat? Worried. Very worried indeed.

Anyway, to take your minds off it, can you tell me the job that each of these fictional characters does?

## POINTLESS QUIZ
1. Atticus Finch
2. Oliver Mellors
3. Hercule Poirot

# 37

# WILL ENGLAND EVER WIN THE WORLD CUP AGAIN?

Every four years it's the same. This time. This time. 'Thirty years of hurt' have quickly become 'forty-seven years of hurt'.

So, will England ever win the World Cup again? English readers are hoping yes, Welsh, Scottish and Irish readers are hoping no. German readers are giggling like schoolchildren.

Let's work it out logically.

Essentially we want to know if England are going to win the World Cup *in our lifetime.* If England win the 2346 World Cup in the Federated States of Post-Nuclear China, with a Phil Neville XVII hat-trick, who cares?

OK, so let's start with the first bit of depressing news.

If you are twenty, then statistically you have only fourteen World Cups left.

If you are forty, then you have nine left.

If you are sixty you have only four left, but no one is going to weep for you because you were around in 1966.

So, will we win any of the next fourteen World Cups? Let's assume:

(a) England will always be around fifth favourite for all World Cup tournaments. Like, say, Spurs.
(b) The World Cup will not be held in England again, due to oligarchs and oil billionaires being the new centre of football power.

OK, let's run the numbers:

1. Exactly half of the World Cups ever played have been won by the favourites. So that's seven of the fourteen World Cups ruled out.
2. A quarter have been won by the second or third favourites. Scrub another 3.5.
3. A European team has never won a World Cup held in South America. Farewell to another two of the fourteen.
4. England never perform at their best in hot and humid

environments, and the Qatar World Cup is just the start of oil-rich countries hosting World Cups. Scratch another three of those fourteen.

5. World Cups are occasionally won on penalties. That rules us out. Another two gone.

6. Lampard and Gerrard can't play together. One gone.

7. We have to assume that Lampard and Gerrard's kids won't be able to play together either. Another one gone.

8. Statistically there will be at least one appalling corruption scandal in the next fourteen World Cups. And you know we won't have had the brains or the money to be behind it. 1.5 gone.

9. We tend to pick the right manager about one time in three. We won't win with the wrong manager, so that's 9.33 World Cups completely out of the question.

10. Bad luck should account for another two or three World Cups. Romeo Beckham's heart-breaking own-goal in the Dubai 2034 final. Let's say 2.5.

So, you just have to do the sums. Even the youngest and perkiest among us have only fourteen World Cups left, and we can see valid statistical reasons that for those fourteen tournaments we will lose 32.83 of them.

So, the bad news for everyone, except the Scottish, the Welsh, the Irish and Baddiel and Skinner's grandchildren, is that England will NEVER win the World Cup again.

# 36

## IS IT OK TO, UM, UH . . . I DON'T REALLY WANT TO SAY THIS OUT LOUD. LET'S JUST SAY THAT THIS ONE IS ABOUT HAVING A WEE. IF YOU DON'T WANT TO READ IT THEN PLEASE MOVE ON

Sometimes I regret asking *Pointless* viewers to send in their own arguments for us to solve. I had fondly imagined them sitting in front of a roaring log fire, a faithful Labrador dozing at their feet, as they tested each other on African capital cities before *Call the Midwife* came on. One would turn to another and posit a discussion that could not immediately be solved, and the other – after a thoughtful suck on a trusty pipe – would suggest turning the issue over to Xander and myself for mediation.

Something like 'Is it ever acceptable to serve Earl Grey tea before luncheon?' or 'Why can you never get the staff these days?'

What we tended to get instead, was this:

Hi Richard,

The argument I would like you to solve is: is it OK to wee in the shower? This is an ongoing debate between me and my flatmates so we would love it if you could come up with some kind of conclusion.

Cheers,
Rachel Adamantos

Oh, Lord, Rachel. Now I have an entirely different mental image in my head, the broad brushstrokes of which involve you and your flatmates reading this book while listening to dubstep in your pants, and probably sniggering over the perfectly innocent expression 'thoughtful suck on a trusty pipe'.

For the record, the following are places in which it is acceptable to wee:

the toilet
a bottle (if on military manoeuvres)
a forest (not at CenterParcs, though)
the sea
a nappy (within reason)

The following are examples of places where it is not acceptable to wee:

church (except a church toilet)
a bottle (if on a date)
a swimming-pool (especially from the diving board)
at the altar
Wolverhampton

As for the shower, Rachel, that's a tricky one. Obviously what one gets up to in one's shower is one's own business. I wouldn't presume to tell any British citizen that they couldn't pee in their own shower any more than I would ever knowingly serve Earl Grey tea before luncheon.

But a shower used by *flatmates*? Or a big family? Or a small family but with Uncle Keith in it? I think that if every single person who is ever likely to use the shower agrees that it is acceptable, then wee away. But even a single vote against means it has to be forbidden. I mean, be honest, you are really, really *near* the loo, aren't you?

So, Rachel, I hope that clears up the issue. And, in the meantime, please think about getting a Labrador, a pipe and a roaring log fire. And would it kill you to put on some trousers?

# 35

# IF YOU COULD LIVE ANYWHERE IN THE WORLD, WHERE WOULD YOU CHOOSE?

One of the classic pub conversations. Or perhaps taverna conversations. If you could live in any country in the world, which would it be? As always, by 'country' I mean a sovereign state that is a member of the UN in its own right.

To help you decide once and for all the best country you could possibly live in, I decided to create a foolproof guide, weighing up the important characteristics you might be looking for in a country. Like the number of palm trees, say, or the ready availability of *Breaking Bad* box-sets.

I have called my foolproof guide, the 'Wellbeing and Lifestyle Evaluation System'. Though, now I look at it, that spells WALES, so I should probably change it. Let's call it 'International Ranking (All Nations)' instead. Problem solved. I have marked every country in the world out of ten on each of the following 10 questions.

1. *Climate*: Sunny, but not *too* hot please. Like Bournemouth on a nice day.
2. *Political stability*: How can I avoid living in Italy?
3. *Do they speak English?*: I'm going to assume that your Serbo-Croat is rusty.
4. *Can you get Jaffa Cakes?*: And, while we're at it, do they have Nando's?
5. *Natural beauty*: Particularly waterfalls, which will make people jealous when I post them on my Facebook page.
6. *Do they have big spiders?* You know, like poisonous ones? That sometimes live under the toilet seat? You know which country I'm talking about.
7. *Would I be terrified if I had to go to hospital?* Or *prison?* Or *the dentist!* Oh, man, just imagine *that*.
8. *The price of a pint and a pie* – or the price of a litre and a brioche, if that's applicable.
9. *Do they like British people?* Surely somewhere still does. Norway?
10. *How easy would it be to watch* Pointless*?*

So, a country such as, say, Central African Republic, scores very highly on climate, natural beauty and the price of a pint, but loses marks when it comes to Jaffa Cakes and Dental Desirability. Overall, then, the Central African Republic scores 47 points, way below somewhere like Sweden, but comfortably higher than France.

Using the index, I have worked out the top five most desirable countries in the world in which to live. Here we go:

5. *United Kingdom.* The UK scored very highly on accessibility of Jaffa Cakes, and lack of poisonous spiders, but lost marks on climate, the price of a pint and the fact that British people *really hate* British people. But a pretty good finish for somewhere you already actually live. Relocation costs minimal.

4. *India.* Lovely weather, cheap booze, endless beauty and impeccable English, but the only place you can watch *Pointless* is in the backstreet betting shops of Mumbai, where millions of rupees change hands every day on whether Carol from Worthing knows any of Rod Stewart's UK top-forty singles.

3. *Republic of Ireland.* Scores identically to the UK, but with cheaper beer.

2. *Canada.* Beautiful, majestic, they love *everyone,* and they have a thriving Jaffa Cake importation industry.

OK, so here's our number one. The answer to the argument 'What's the best country in the world to live in?' You're not going to like the answer any more than I do, but feel free to do the sums yourself. I've checked and double-checked them. The best country to live in is . . .

1. *Germany*

I know, bad news, right? But think about it:

(a) Beautiful summers and wonderful landscapes (remember the lovely hills Steve McQueen drove his motorbike over in *The Great Escape*).
(b) Political stability going back, ooh, fifty-eight years or so (since the end of *The Great Escape* pretty much).
(c) Perfect English (remember that Nazi officer saying, 'Good luck,' in *The Great Escape*?). Barges full of Jaffa Cakes drifting down the Rhine, no scary bugs.
(d) *Pointless* on satellite.
(e) And, best of all, they *have* to pretend to like British people due to their past misdemeanours (upon which we will not dwell here).

So, like it or not, our answer is GERMANY.

# 34

# ARE MENSA MEMBERS DEAD BRAINY?

So there's this thing, isn't there, called MENSA. It's a clever club that only really, really clever people can be in. And what's the point of it? Well, you get a monthly newsletter, a membership card, and the opportunity to participate in club activities – pleasures familiar to anyone who has ever belonged to something exclusive and special, be it the Brownies, the Matt Bianco fan club, or UKIP. You pay to sit a MENSA-approved IQ test, they send it off to be marked and after a little while, if you scored highly enough to get into the top two per cent (that's the top two per cent of all living humans, from Stephen Hawking to the cast of *The Only Way Is Essex*), you can enrol. And within days you will receive the famous membership card, which you presumably then spend the rest of your life producing in pubs to settle bets.

Are members of MENSA especially brainy, though? It's a tricky question to answer, though happily it's multiple-choice:

(a) yes, (b) no, (c) I don't know, but, look, I've got a MENSA membership card. Well, they must be brainy to a point because they have to pass the test to join.* But then there's that other thing you can be part of, isn't there, called Normal Life, and that also gives you an opportunity to shine. You don't get a membership card in Normal Life as such, but your braininess can be quietly evident in the decisions you've taken, and the career and friends you've made over the years. Sometimes these careers can even be in academia where you can use your braininess to further human endeavour. So, it looks like we've uncovered two types of braininess: one that likes the trappings of being an acknowledged brainbox and the other that just gets on with being good at what it's good at.

There's something about the name MENSA too. It's Latin. And Latin sounds clever. Knowing a bit of Latin makes even Boris Johnson appear less of an idiot. So, when coming up with a clever name for their clever organisation, the clever people at MENSA chose a Latin word. If MENSA sounds a bit mental to you, well, the Latin for 'mind' is *mens*, so we're in the right area. Of course, if anyone called their organisation of clever people 'Mens', they'd be accused of sexism before you can say Jack (or Jancis) Robinson. And, more to

---

* Although, to be honest, if I were in MENSA I would find it difficult not to wave through anyone who was prepared to send me their bank details but then I'm sure they're much, much, much more scrupulous than I am.

the point, you'd be denying yourself the opportunity to persuade 50 per cent of the world's population to pay up the membership fees. So, with 'Mens' a nonstarter, they clearly opted for something that sounded Latin and mental, but wasn't: MENSA. It's Latin for 'table'. Being clever sorts, some of them knew this, so they deliberately incorporated it into their logo. They now claim this represents the fact that they're a 'round-table' kind of organisation, a meeting of equals. The less generous of you might think it's fitting for a bunch of people who, IQ aside, can be as thick as planks.

In the cult TV series *The Prisoner*, Patrick McGoohan's character would always shout, 'I am not a number, I am a free man.' MENSA members swing dangerously the other way, verging closer to a cry of 'I'm not a man, I'm a number.' Are MENSA members dead brainy? I'm going to say yes. But they're also a bit 'brain-deady'. And they'll never be as clever as the people who run the bow-tie concessions at MENSA conventions.**

......................................................................................................

** The lawyers for this book, who are much brainier than I am, have pointed out that MENSA calls itself a 'not-for-profit organisation' and suggest it might be a good idea for me to draw attention to this fact. So, I'm delighted to repeat that MENSA is a not-for-profit organisation ... which suggests they're not as smart as I thought they were.

The following famous people are all reputed to have been MENSA members, can you tell us who they are from the clues?

## POINTLESS QUIZ

1. Author of the 1983 book *Castaway*
2. Army officer who commanded Desert Storm
3. She was 'Private Benjamin' in the 1980 film
4. Richard Whiteley's co-host on *Countdown*
5. Russian-born author who devised the 'Three Laws of Robotics'
6. Played 'The Jerk' in 1979 and 'The Man With Two Brains' in 1983
7. Played Drago in *Rocky IV*
8. Co-starred with Susan Sarandon in *Thelma & Louise*
9. Directed 1994 film *Pulp Fiction*
10. Inventor of the C5 electric vehicle
11. Presented *Live & Kicking* with Zoë Ball
12. Won 100m breaststroke gold medal at the Seoul Olympics

# 33

# SHOULD I BOTHER VOTING?
# THEY'RE ALL THE SAME

1. Yes, you should.
2. No, they're not.

# 32

# SHOULD I GET A DEGREE OR NOT?

Let's think about this one. What exactly do you want from your course at university? Apart, that is, from a crippling debt. Is it the immersion in an academic faculty devoted to the furtherance of knowledge? Is it the continuance of a school-like curriculum and the reassuring cycle of syllabus and exam? Or is it the fact that you're buying another three or four years of getting up in time to watch *Pointless*, drinking too much, and not having to go out and get a job? There is absolutely nothing wrong with any of these reasons and, in most people's cases, the honest answer is probably a mix of all three. But with the cost of tuition going up and the value of so many degrees coming down, it is genuinely worth taking the time to assess the value of a degree to you. Below is an easy-to-use table to help you. If you answer yes to any of the qualifiers in the left-hand column you can find your definitive answer in the right-hand column opposite.

| Qualifier | Should you get a degree or not? |
|---|---|
| Have you already begun your course? | MIGHT AS WELL |
| Do you intend to work hard? | YES |
| Are you so damned clever you don't even *need* to work hard? | YES |
| Do you intend to play sport at uni? | YES |
| Are you planning to have the best time ever? | YES |
| Are you prepared to sleep with absolutely anyone to get what you want in life? | NO |
| Do you want to leave off studying until a life sentence for murder reintroduces you to the joy of libraries? | NO |
| Would you rather develop your intellect so you can commit the perfect murder without getting caught and going to prison? | YES |
| Do you want to become a university don? | PROBABLY |
| Is your course a foreign language, forcing you to take a year's extra 'study', lounging on a foreign beach? | YES |

| | |
|---|---|
| Does your father have millions in the bank and a dodgy ticker? | WHY BOTHER? |
| Are you a virgin? | YES |
| Have you read *Brideshead Revisited* and now want to flounce about in a light suit while clutching a teddy bear? | NO, STAY AWAY |
| Do you want to spend your middle age watching *University Challenge* and getting one or two answers right? | DON'T EXPECT A DEGREE TO HELP |
| Do you currently live at home, with no foreseeable way out? | YES |
| Do you want to be sneered at by locals who wish they didn't live in a university town? | YES |
| Do you want to become a reality-show celebrity? | NO |
| Do you want to end up with a lot of unread books that no one else wants? | YES |
| Do you want to live in a house with a bunch of people who, in later life, you'll either forget, form a start-up company with, fall out big-time with, envy as they do better than you, look down on as you do better than them, or wish you'd shagged? | YES |

# 31

# SHOULD YOU STAND STILL ON ESCALATORS?

OK, time for another argument submitted by a loyal *Pointless* viewer, Mark Rea.

Well, I *say* 'loyal'. If I really think about it, he might not be loyal at all. I mean, I can't actually see through the camera, so I don't know if he's sometimes missed a day. Or if he's ever taken a phone call during one of my rounds on nineteenth-century literature. But I trust Mark. I'm sure he'd tell me if he was seeing another show, wouldn't he?

Mark writes:

The pointless argument I have most with my wife is, 'Why do you stop walking on escalators?' She insists on standing still on escalators and moving walkways, and having never lived in London, doesn't even stand on the right.

Well, first, if that's the most pointless argument you have with your wife, I'd say you have a pretty awesome marriage. She is a keeper.

Second, are you sure you want me to solve it once and for all? What if it gets replaced with a worse argument, like 'Why do you always clear your Internet history, Mark?' or 'Mark! Would it *kill you* to flush every once in a while?'

But if you're prepared for those consequences let's get this one cleared up.

Your logic is impeccable. Escalators are installed in place of stairs. Your wife would have to walk up those stairs. The escalator is designed to make that walk easier, not to give you a well-earned rest on your gruelling twenty-second climb from the ground floor to the first floor of Debenhams.

Equally a travelator is designed to get you to an airport gate quicker, not to let you stand stock-still, leaving your cases in the way of people who have continued walking (me, say).

So, by that logic, she should walk. You win the argument, and you can wander around the house with a well-earned feeling of superiority, right up until she asks, 'Whose turn is it to put the bins out?'

But, but, but, but, but. Escalators are not really a *replacement* for stairs. They tend to be in *really big* places, don't they? For example, the longest single escalator in the world is in the Park Pobedy Metro Station in Moscow, is 740 steps long, and takes nearly three minutes to ride. And they only have travelators at airports because your plane lands about seven miles from your bags, then this distance is doubled because you endlessly have to keep going round corners for no reason whatsoever. Even the hardiest and fittest of passengers who confidently stride down the first few travelators tend to put their feet up by the fifteenth or sixteenth. Here's a plan, airports. We'll stay by the plane and you can put all our bags on the travelators and send them to us.

The only reason department stores, shopping centres, airports, tube stations and the like can be built on such a massive scale is that they have worked out a way of making it humanly possible for customers to get around without having to be wrapped in foil and handed a Mars Bar when they reach their destination. They're *specifically designed* to give you a rest (like the 'false-flats' built for horses pulling coaches up steep hills in previous centuries). If you don't want to rest, that is your choice and will certainly keep you fit, and get you where you're going quicker, but if your wife chooses to stand, she is well within her right to do so.

Or, to put it another way, I'm guessing you let her stand still in a lift, don't you?

Sorry, Mark. I hope this doesn't affect your loyalty, and at least the subject of your Internet history should be safe for a while longer.

# 30

## CHICKEN OR BEEF?

The big one. Even though it's barely half eleven when the lunch-trolley comes down the aisle, the enticing smell of hot food and foil has got to you. You've got three hours till touchdown in Seville. You've read and reread the inflight magazine and still can't quite convince yourself you need a new watch, or a furry replica aeroplane, and you're suddenly so hungry you could – in the unfortunate words of an expression that long pre-dates the meat-supply scandal of early 2013 – eat a horse. You have a fraction of a second to decide which of the food-styles on offer you will spend the next seven or eight minutes trying to coerce onto the feeble tines of a plastic baby fork, then you must speak. The more alert will, of course, have known what the choices were from the minute the respective face and arse of Peter and Lee-Anne rolled into view with their hot trolley a few rows ahead, but don't think for a moment that this is one of those answers you can get from straining to listen to what others are saying.

This isn't a pub quiz. It's down to you. You can't cheat Chicken or Beef. Which is it to be? Cluck or Moo? Grain or Cud? Which? I can't hear you! WHICH? As George Orwell would most certainly have put it: 'Two legs bad, four legs equally bad.'

OK. Well, let's knock off the easy one first. Are you Hindu? If so, I'd probably go, 'Chicken.'

In fact the first wave of rationale says, 'Chicken,' every time. It's a lean meat – good for the weight conscious (which, let's face it, is all of us – especially on a flight to Seville, City of Marmalade).* Plus we've all had a longer relationship with chicken than we have with beef. We knew our way around that bird before we knew anything about the yeasty brownness of the bovine. It's a first-base comfort meat (as they would almost certainly say in the advert, if they had to advertise chicken – which they don't because WE ALREADY LOVE CHICKEN),** whereas beef is heavy, complex and forbidding. And has horns. So at this stage I'd say chicken has taken an early lead.

..................................................................................................

* It's probably called this. ('City of Marmalade' is a title also claimed by Glasgow, home of the sixties band that got to number one with a cover of 'Ob-La-Di, Ob-La-Da'.)

** There has never been an ex-cricketer with a poultry-based nickname voicing some baffling cartoon of himself in order to big up the meat of a hen. I've checked.

Oh, but hang on a sec. There are one or two issues with chicken breast (assuming it really is breast and, given the scope for misunderstanding, you don't really want to be asking Lee-Anne whether the breasts are real or not). Isn't it always going to be dry – especially in a pressurised-cabin scenario – and a little bit woolly? While that beef is more likely to be nice and juicy thanks to its lavish all-round fatti-ness. Maybe we'll go for the beef after all.

Whoa there! Stop! The chicken comes with mini carrots and what appears to be piped mash. That's top-notch babyfood in any man's language. Meanwhile the beef seems to be accompanied by tiny onions, peas, and some kind of mush. What is that? Celeriac? Turnip? Last week's chicken? Euch.

But – time out – let's just think for a moment about the anonymous sweat-shop that churns out thousands of these meals a day – with no lunch break for the workers (at their request). While the strong likelihood is that they send their beef and chicken buyers out, like men from Del Monte, to scour the land looking for the very best free-range, organic meat, there is still an infinitesimally small chance that they might just buy any old crap at the lowest market price they can find. Ridiculously unlikely though this obviously is, espe-cially in the cuddly, un-cutthroat business that is air travel, we should probably still factor it in. After all, these are people willing to accept a bribe of a couple of quid to let you jump the boarding queue.

Now, for me, the chicken isn't looking so clever. I'd rather eat a knock-down quadruped that has at least lived outside and eaten grass (or sugar lumps) than a knock-down chicken, which has probably been raised in a dark box and fed on alcopops and bits of other chickens.

So the proper answer in this case is 'Go for the veggie option or eat as much as you can before you leave home.' However, if you ask me 'Chicken or beef?', with a plastic baby knife to my throat, my answer would be . . .

BEEF.

What do you mean you're out of beef? OK, then . . .

CHICKEN.

# 29

# ARE BRITISH SPORTS BETTER THAN AMERICAN SPORTS?

**\*\*\* AUTHOR'S WARNING \*\*\***
FOR A NUMBER OF REASONS IT IS IMPORTANT
THAT YOU DO NOT READ THE FOLLOWING IF YOU
ARE A HUGE CRICKET FAN WITH ACCESS TO
WEAPONRY, A HISTORY OF GRUDGES AND MY
ADDRESS. IF THIS SOUNDS LIKE *YOU* PLEASE
TURN TO THE NEXT ARGUMENT IMMEDIATELY.
I PROMISE YOU THERE IS NOTHING UPSETTING
ABOUT CRICKET THERE.

Have they gone? Good. I'm *totally* going to say something upsetting about cricket.

OK, I'm going to need you all to come on a journey with me now. Not an *actual* journey: the logistics of that would be impossible. We're going, instead, on a journey of the imagination. If we're truly going to compare British sports with

American sports we need to be utterly objective, so we have to forget we're British for a moment. Ready?

To become un-British I need you to do one of the following things:

(a) Have cake for breakfast.
(b) Wear an enormous rucksack and walk slowly in front of me down a busy shopping street.
(c) Win the World Cup.

Done one of those? OK, you are now not British. Let's proceed to look objectively at British and US sports.

### FOOTBALL V. AMERICAN FOOTBALL

I think we can all instantly see that our football is better than American football. Whether you like it or not, it's the biggest sport in the world, it fires hearts and minds wherever it's played, and provides wonderful global role models, such as Wayne Rooney. There are 227 countries* in the world, and if they were to vote on which was better, the score would be 226–1. Or maybe 225–2: you can never *really* trust the Fijians.

...............................................................................

\* As always, by 'country' I mean a sovereign state that is a member of the UN in its own right.

## CRICKET V. BASEBALL

OK, here's where I really get into trouble. Remember that you are *not* British. Take another pinch of that paprika. Ready? Now, take a long, hard look at cricket without the emotional attachment. I mean, honestly I do love cricket, but I can't get over the central issue that the purest form of the game takes five days to play and regularly ends in a draw because *there's not enough time to finish it*. Baseball, meanwhile, has taken the basic principles of cricket,

(a) Throwing a ball at a stick
(b) Running when you manage to hit it really hard
(c) Being allowed to have a drink while you watch

and has distilled them into a thrilling evening's entertainment, which now has behind it a rich and evocative history woven deep into the fabric of the American story. So don't hate me, but this one goes to baseball.

## ICE HOCKEY V. SNOOKER

Ice hockey has non-stop visceral action, blindingly fast reflexes, extraordinary physical power and almost endless fights. Snooker has two men, who last saw natural daylight in 1994, rubbing chalk onto a bit of wood in a provincial theatre while John Virgo says, 'But where's the cue ball going?' One clear winner here.

But fortunately my un-Britishness is wearing off, so the winner is snooker. Because I love it, my nan and grandad loved it, and I don't care what the rest of the world thinks. Ice hockey is just some Canadian men falling over, and none of them is even Cliff Thorburn.

The other great thing about US sports is, of course, those names they give all of their teams. The Arizona Diamondbacks, for example, is cooler than Swindon Town.

Here's a little quiz. I'm going to give you the names of American football and baseball teams that play in a particular city. But which city? Before you start could you just check that Uncle Keith isn't on his way round to my house with a cricket bat?

## POINTLESS QUIZ

1. 49Ers/Giants
2. Texans/Astros
3. Bears/Cubs
4. Eagles/Phillies
5. Seahawks/Mariners
6. Rams/Cardinals
7. Redskins/Nationals
8. Raiders/Athletics
9. Dolphins/Marlins
10. Browns/Indians
11. Chiefs/Royals
12. Steelers/Pirates

# 28

## SENT FROM MY IPAD – USEFUL OR TEDIOUS?

If you're receiving an email, do you care remotely how it was typed up and sent? No, of course not. No email can be sweetened or soured by the details of its e-posting, be that message 'Got a couple of tickets for Wimbledon final, interested?' to 'OMG, I'm pregnant. What shall we do?' And, anyway, the sign-off might as well say, 'Sent from the back of a cab' or 'Dashed off awkwardly while queuing at Boots' for all it tells you about your correspondent's concentration on the job in hand. Or it'll tell you too much – 'Sent from the bathroom, between dump and wipe'. Besides, what are you supposed to do with this information? Do I go around saying, 'That sentence just came from my mouth'? No.*

Maybe it was suggested by an elderly relative of Steve Jobs

........................................................................

* Oh, actually, hang on, yes, sometimes I do but I'm new to ventriloquism and I just worry that people won't 'get' it.

as an old-fashioned courtesy that would appeal to the sort of people who like sending letters on hotel writing paper. You know that flimsy stuff that sits under the room service menu in the drawer of the desk with the obsolete modem connection on it? Yeah, that's for writing letters on to your great-aunt Dahlia to say you'll be getting the mid-day post-chaise and to expect you at seven so prepare a maid, or perhaps to your amanuensis back at the club so he can let the king know there are grave misdeeds afoot. But even then Aunt D is as likely as not to look at the paper and say, 'Sent from the Hôtel Le Bristol, eh? Like I give a crap. Flash git. Oh, and, Carruthers, prepare a maid.'

Actually the truth is grimmer than that. The 'Sent from my iPad' message is there for one reason and one reason only. It advertises iPads. It tells people that other people have iPads. It repeats the word 'iPad' so many times that after a while it's impossible not to have the word 'iPad' in your list of Top Ten Words on the Brain. This was what made the late Steve Jobs a genius. He saw a cunning way of promoting his product in every email sent, smuggling his odious iSpam into even the tiniest 'Ta', 'See you later' or 'Are you sure I'm the dad?' I just hope, wherever he's ended up, be it Heaven or Hell, he has emblazoned across his forehead 'Sent from Earth'.

The good news is that there's a way of removing it. Open 'Settings', select 'Mail, Contacts, Calendar', scroll down and select 'Signature', then edit your signature to say something else. But, let's face it, even that is a chore that we could all do without.

No, there's no two ways about it. 'Sent from my iPad' is tedious.

# 27

# IS IT BETTER TO BE UNDER THIRTY OR OVER SEVENTY?

It is commonly perceived that to be young is the finest state of being there is. The strength and energy, the optimism, the easy grace. All those opportunities, the plans, the flings, the long, beautiful paths that stretch ahead. Whereas we fear age. We're terrified of it. Immobility, mortality, invisibility.

But I don't buy this for a second. Sure, being young these days has the same wonderful benefits as ever. Your story is unwritten and the possibilities endless. But, let's not forget, you can't afford a house, every night you have to choose between about seven hundred types of lager or even pear cider, for goodness' sake, and you still haven't produced a band half as good as the Beatles or Nirvana.

The life of the under-thirties is an endless whirlwind of way too much choice and way too little money. And who wants to be trapped in an endless whirlwind of *any* kind? If nothing else, it would play havoc with that haircut all the under-thirties seem to have.

So, to the old. The over-seventies. Is it really as bad as we fear? Or are we, as I suspect, simply the victims of an elaborate con-trick?

My mum was a primary-school teacher until she retired. She now leads what seems from the outside to be an extraordinary life of leisure, involving just drinking with friends, playing cards and asking me if I've ever met Stephen Fry. I can honestly say that if, in twenty years' time, I discover a series of documents proving that my mum and her circle of friends spent the whole of their seventies taking heroin I will not be at all surprised. At the very least, I'm sure they're up to *something*.

They combine a fierce independence with a remarkable ability to appear frail when something they don't really want to do crops up. Every single one of them has a child, grandchild, nephew, niece or the son of their local newsagent, who will gladly set up a Freeview box for them, or spend two hours on the line to the broadband helpdesk. We know full well you can do this yourself, you thrash us at *Countdown*, for goodness' sake. You've just lived long enough to know it'll be a bit of a pain and you could probably get someone else to do it.

The big trouble is that the over-seventies are all so *charming*. The charm that comes with not being in a hurry, and not giving the slightest toss what you think about them. And they have an air of wisdom that comes with age. They're not *actually* wise, of course: they're as worryingly stupid as they were at sixteen or twenty-eight or thirty-nine. They have just learned that the secret of appearing wiser is simply to say less.

There is not a lot wrong, for example, with the following as the timetable for your day:

6 a.m.: For some reason get up.

6.30 a.m.: Nice cup of tea.

7 a.m.: Go to the gym. No, only kidding! The *gym*! Who cares? I've got a *titanium hip*! You go to the gym, I'm going back to bed! Hahahahaha!

8 a.m.: Get up again. Feel a sense of calm and serenity, which comes with knowing that everyone else is in a traffic jam on the way to work while I'm looking at a bird table and thinking it's about time I had some toast.

9.15 a.m.: Watch *Heir Hunters* and *Homes Under the Hammer*.

10.30 a.m.: Deirdre comes round for coffee. Let her tell me about her grandson for ten minutes, in return for listening to me talk about my grandson for ten minutes. Hearing aids off.

11.30 a.m.: Plot with friends. (What on earth are you planning? You know we'll find out, don't you?)

12.30 p.m.: Is it lunchtime already?

1.30 p.m.: Snooze followed by *Morse* followed by *Lewis* followed by snooze.

3 p.m.: Get a bus into town. FOR FREE. Then have a Starbucks, which is essentially being funded by the taxpayer.

5 p.m.: Dinnertime. Watch *Pointless*. Effortlessly answer everything, until there's a round I don't know about, at which moment pretend either my hearing or eyesight is playing up: 'I found it very difficult to hear the questions in that round about Lady Gaga.'

6 p.m.: Drinking with Marjory, Bill, some nice woman Bill appears to have picked up on the bus but whose name I missed and now it's too late to ask, Elaine, Colin and Colin's friend Alf, whom no one is sure about yet.

7 p.m.: Drinking turns into playing cards.

9 p.m.: An ITV drama with David Tennant.

10 p.m.: Cup of tea.

10.30 p.m.: Bed.

You'd take that, wouldn't you? Especially after a life in which you just about dodged the Second World War and, unless Kin Jong-un gets his skates on, you're going to miss the Third World War. And you managed to buy for six thousand pounds a house that is now so expensive that anyone under thirty would have to sell their internal organs to get a deposit for it.

There are downsides, of course, chief among them declining health or mobility. But the mental and emotional upsides of age are mammoth. This is largely thanks to perspective: the true understanding of what matters and what doesn't. And the type of sixth sense about human nature that comes with watching *Morse* and *Lewis* every day.

Mortality casts a long shadow. Funerals start to become as commonplace as trips to IKEA are for the under-thirties. And they are occasionally as harrowing. But that's the circle of life. We're all on it somewhere, and we'll all be getting off in time. It's just that you have that lovely free pass of yours.

Clearly if you're under thirty you're also likely to be over seventy at some point so, strictly speaking, that's the best of both worlds. But if we were just to take a day at random and ask who's having the most fun, enjoying the most peace and living life the way it should be lived, my vote goes to the over-seventies.

# 26

# IS GRAMMAR IMPORTANT?

No, it aren't. And nor speling as well.

Syntax, on the other hand, is one of those things a knowledge of without which one would find sentences unnavigable.

# 25

## WHAT ARE THE BEST AND WORST COVER VERSIONS OF ALL TIME?

Remember how furious your dad was when One Direction released their cover version of Blondie's 'One Way Or Another' and the Undertones' 'Teenage Kicks'? Oh, man, he went *nuts*.

It's just the sort of thing dads are supposed to get cross about, of course. Dads are designed to spend most of their time furious that either

(a) One Direction have 'ruined, just absolutely *ruined*' 'Teenage Kicks', or that

(b) Sunderland have lost again.

But don't forget that all the time he's furious about those things, he isn't noticing that you've got a tattoo. Result.*

.....................................................................................

\* By the way, it looks cool.

Dads are idiots. I assume I don't have to present any evidence for this. We all just know, don't we? I mean they're *lovely* and everything, but they *are* idiots.

A friend of mine (a dad, naturally) complained a couple of years ago that Alexandra Burke from *The X Factor* had 'ruined, just absolutely *ruined*' Jeff Buckley's 'Hallelujah'. Forgetting, of course, that Jeff Buckley's 'Hallelujah' was itself a cover version, of Leonard Cohen's 'Hallelujah'. And it was better.

Dads would be furious to hear that anyone had covered Elvis Presley's 'Hound Dog', Aretha Franklin's 'Respect', Marvin Gaye's 'Heard It Through The Grapevine' or The Beatles' 'Twist & Shout'. But, as the brighter (i.e. mums) among you will have worked out, they were all cover versions in the first place.

Some of the greatest performers of all time, from David Bowie to Prince to Elton John, have had their songs performed much, much better by others.

To prove to your dad how awesome cover versions can be, why not put together this playlist for him? The top twelve cover versions of all time, compiled by me with the help of cool mums, unmarried men and married men without kids. It was supposed to be a top ten but I couldn't bear the arguing any more and had to sneak a couple more in to keep Keeley and Mark happy.

1. 'HALLELUJAH' – Jeff Buckley
2. 'ONE' – Johnny Cash (great U2 track, made even greater by the Man In Black)
3. 'JEALOUS GUY' – Roxy Music (a fitting tribute to John Lennon)
4. 'ONLY LOVE CAN BREAK YOUR HEART' – St Etienne (lovely Neil Young ballad becomes gorgeous electronic ballad)
5. 'UMBRELLA' – Manic Street Preachers (Dad will like this one. The Manics make over Rihanna. They also do a cracking cover of 'Suicide Is Painless')
6. 'MODERN LOVE' – Last Town Chorus (eighties David Bowie stripped back and slowed up. See also Nirvana's version of 'The Man Who Sold The World')
7. 'TWIST & SHOUT' – The Beatles (originally recorded by the Top Notes, and included by the Beatles at the last moment as an afterthought on their début album, *Please Please Me*)
8. 'DON'T LEAVE ME THIS WAY' – The Communards (the definitive version of the track, originally recorded by Harold Melvin & the Blue Notes)
9. 'ALWAYS ON MY MIND' – Pet Shop Boys (Christmas number one. And if your dad prefers the Elvis original, let him know that it wasn't the original. Brenda Lee released it first)
10. 'A NEW ENGLAND' – Kirsty MacColl (Kirsty shows what a wonderful songwriter Billy Bragg is. She also did a mean version of 'Days' by the Kinks)

11. 'OOPS I DID IT AGAIN' – Richard Thompson (folk troubadour reworks Britney Spears)
12. 'HOUNDS OF LOVE' – Futureheads (Kate Bush does a cracking 'Rocket Man' by Elton John, but our final track is one of hers, updated by Sunderland's Futureheads)

I promise you, your dad will love this playlist. But given that he has now noticed your tattoo, but still hasn't found out that your new boyfriend has a motorbike, let's keep him happy with a list of the five *worst* cover versions of all time.

5. 'SMELLS LIKE TEEN SPIRIT' – Take That (yes, *really*. A very rare wrong move from Gary Barlow)
4. 'SONG 2' – Robbie Williams (a less rare wrong move from Robbie Williams)
3. 'TEENAGE KICKS' – One Direction (I honestly like One Direction, and I'll let them off 'One Way Or Another', but on this one your dad is right, and in ten years' time you will be apologising to him)
2. '911 IS A JOKE' – Duran Duran (it turns out that Duran Duran were not the right band to cover this fiercely provocative Public Enemy classic)
1. 'FAIRYTALE OF NEW YORK' – Ronan Keating and Marie Brennan (please, seeing as it's Christmas, do not try to find this on YouTube. I promise you'll regret it. Wait! *Wait*, where are you *going*? Noooooooo!)

Assuming you've just ruined Christmas by disobeying my instructions (isn't it *terrible*?), let's see if we can calm everybody down with these questions. In each instance the second act covered a track that had also been recorded by the first act. Name the tracks!

## POINTLESS QUIZ

1. Soft Cell/Marilyn Manson
2. Guns N' Roses/Sheryl Crow
3. Weather Girls/Geri Halliwell
4. The Pretenders/Girls Aloud
5. Nancy Sinatra/Jessica Simpson
6. Dusty Springfield/White Stripes
7. The Righteous Brothers/Robson & Jerome
8. Oasis/Mike Flowers Pops
9. Shirley Bassey/Tom Jones
10. Bee Gees/Steps
11. Nina Simone/Muse
12. Harold Faltermeyer/Crazy Frog
13. Nilsson/Mariah Carey
14. Don McLean/Madonna

# 24

# ARE MY CHILDREN ENGLISH?

Don't forget that this book has a number of purposes.

(a) Solving all arguments ever.
(b) Helping you to organise a quiz with your family where you have already secretly looked up the answers, without realising that they have secretly looked up the answers too.
(c) Propping up a table.
(d) Somewhere to keep the tartan bookmark that Elaine from the office somehow thought would make a nice present from her holiday. Even though she knows you love whisky.
(e) Helping you to look super-hot while reading it on a train. I guarantee you will pull.*

.................................................................................

* Guarantee imaginary.

But, of course, one of its purposes is to solve the arguments of loyal *Pointless* viewers, however misguided they may be.

Here is a message we received from Katherine Rigby:

> I am English. My partner was born in Scotland but has one Scottish and one Welsh parent. Our children were born in Aberdeen. I say they are more English than Scottish (because if they'd been born in Barbados that wouldn't make them Barbadian). He says not. Who is right?

Oh, Katherine, you may not like this answer. Your calculation is that if you are English, and your husband half Scottish and half Welsh, then your children are half English, quarter Welsh and quarter Scottish?

But what do you mean when you say your parents are English and your husband's parents are Welsh and Scottish? You're saying that your parents were born in England, and your husband's parents were born in Wales and Scotland. That's what makes them English, Welsh and Scottish.

I was born in Essex and I will always be an Essex boy, even though I am not orange and don't own my own nightclub.

Your children were born in Aberdeen. And Aberdeen is in Scotland. That's why you can see those mountains, and why everybody outside is so friendly. That makes them Scottish. One hundred per cent Scottish. If they *had been* born in Barbados (which, incidentally, would be cool) they would be 100 per cent Barbadian.

But don't worry about losing the argument. Your kids are very lucky to be Scottish. They'll never have the stress of wondering if Scotland will win the World Cup, and everybody will always love their accent. Which means they'll be able to pull on trains even when not reading this book.

# 23

# SHOULD I BELIEVE MY HOROSCOPE?

Seventeen per cent of British people believe in horoscopes. That is more people than voted Lib Dem. And *they* sort of run the country.

So, should we believe in them? They are vague, muddled, almost always wrong, and if you rely on them in any meaningful way, they will let you down. But enough about Lib Dems, let's discuss horoscopes.

The answer all depends on which star sign you are. So, for this one particular argument I have provided twelve separate, very different answers.

ARIES (21 March–19 April)
No, you shouldn't believe your horoscope. They're nonsense.

TAURUS (20 April–20 May)
Neither should you. Come *on*.

GEMINI (21 May–20 June)
The sign of the twins. *Neither of you* should believe
your horoscope. Unless you are Jedward, in which
case 'Venus is in the ascendant, meaning that now
would be a good time to quit the music business.'

CANCER (21 June–22 July)
You are sensitive, but can be strong when things you
love are challenged. Me too. Everyone is. That's why
they tell you that in your horoscope.

LEO (23 July–22 August)
You will soon meet a stranger. He will tell you your
horoscope. Don't believe him. And don't buy any of
his heather. If it really *was* lucky he'd be on a beach
in Barbados, not selling heather outside a bus station.

VIRGO (23 August–22 September)
The number seven is very important to you. As it is
to everyone. Without it, six would bump into eight.

LIBRA (23 September–22 October)
You have a natural balance in life. Your horoscope is
the perfect balance of well-meaning nonsense and
cash-generating phone lines.

SCORPIO (23 October–21 November)
You have eight legs and live in a web of silk.


SAGITTARIUS (22 November–21 December)
You share a star sign with Richard from *Pointless*, so
you are tall and you also need to go to the shop for
milk as soon as you have finished writing this.


CAPRICORN (22 December–19 January)
What are you, a goat? Or is that Taurus? It is possible
that your birthday is on Christmas Day. Wow, what's
that like? Or a birthday on Boxing Day? Is that worse
or better?


AQUARIUS (20 January–18 February)
You have a Q in your name so you score the most
points in Scrabble. It would also get rid of two Us,
and they can be hard to get rid of.


PISCES (19 February–20 March)
Hey, fish face, don't believe your horoscope.


I hope this has helped. If you need more information about
why you should ignore your horoscope please ring 0879
987768 (calls cost £8.60 per minute, minimum call 17
minutes).

For seven years, astrologer Joan Quigley effectively ran the USA. After President Reagan was shot, Joan advised Nancy, and Nancy advised Ronnie. Her advice controlled everything at the White House from the date of the president's cancer surgery to his attitude towards the Soviet Union.

Some believe that there are actually thirteen houses in the zodiac, with Arachne (the 'spider' or 'weaver') tucked between Taurus and Gemini.

# 22

# WHICH IS THE BEST CURRENCY IN THE WORLD?

You can develop an attachment to currencies for all manner of different reasons – and not just because, in every single case, it's money. Your own country's currency, for example, is an obvious one to favour. And the euro is one that's hard to like – unless you're really, really into *Schadenfreude*.* Or perhaps you might look kindly on currencies that have the most colourful banknotes such as those of São Tomé and Príncipe, bedecked with birds and presidents in such gaudy colours that, for a split second, their people can forget just how poor they really are. And what about those countries that have the highest denominations?**

..............................................................................................

* Odd how, in this context, the Germans should have the perfect word.
** It's a pleasing sign of quaint UK custom that taxi drivers and shopkeepers in the capital still get quite sweaty about fifty-pound notes when this is, in fact, an absurdly low value for our highest

Then again you may feel you prefer those currencies that perform most reliably in the world markets, currencies you never have to touch, whose existence is primarily on computer screens or talked about in that bit of the news when the mind automatically shuts off; currencies that avoid the melodramatic highs and lows of Latin American countries, or the capricious wiggles of the former Soviet economies; solid currencies like the Swiss franc that bob along with no tossing of curls, just the dogged consistency of one of those slightly sinister mechanical cobbler puppets in the windows of key-cutting shops.

We have devised an entirely scientific means of applying all these factors and have thereby arrived at the conclusion that our favourite world currency is the magnificent Vietnamese dong.

........................

denomination banknote. Especially compared to the 500-euro note, the 10,000-dollar bill in the USA, or Hungary's 100-quintillion-pengö note issued in 1946. Try getting change out of that at one thirty in the morning.

Actually, shopkeepers don't mind at all. It gives them a lovely opportunity to get out their 'fraud detector' pens and get all CSI with you. The fact that the only thing these pens can detect is a forgery made on a colour photocopier doesn't seem to diminish their zeal in any way.

Can you tell us the currencies of the following countries?

## POINTLESS QUIZ

1. Thailand
2. India
3. Spain
4. Croatia
5. Hungary
6. Poland
7. Mexico
8. Kenya
9. Switzerland
10. Tunisia
11. South Korea
12. United States

## POINTLESS FACTS

Rampant inflation in 1946 Hungary led to the introduction of the banknote with the highest denomination ever, the 100 million billion pengö, worth about twenty American pennies.

In 1997, when Joseph Mobutu was overthrown in Zaïre (now the Democratic Republic of the Congo), the new government simply cut his image out of the existing currency.

# 21

# IS THE EARTH BEING RULED BY A GLOBAL ÉLITE OF SHAPE-SHIFTING LIZARDS?

I don't know if this is a new argument to you, but the idea that the world is secretly run by enormous lizards has genuinely been gaining much traction in recent years. It has been popularised mainly by David Icke, so it's best to assume that there's something in it. Icke summarises his theory thus: 'Humanity is actually under the control of dinosauroid-like alien reptiles who must consume human blood to maintain their human appearance.'

These shape-shifting reptiles were originally extra-terrestrial, but have been on earth for many thousands of years. They live, for the main part, in a series of underground tunnels and caverns. Or sometimes Kettering. The ultimate goal of this global reptile élite is world domination and the microchipping of the human population. Sort of like if your local vet got ideas above her station.

Icke has accused many prominent people of being 'reptoids', including George Bush Sr, George W. Bush, Queen Elizabeth II, the late Queen Mother, Al Gore and Kris Kristofferson.

But *are* they? Are we *really* being ruled by enormous space newts?

I mean, sure, we've all suspected *Kris Kristofferson* of being an alien dinosauroid. But George Bush? He always seemed so normal.

But here's the thing. Icke has repeated these allegations *many* times, in public and in print. And for Icke the final proof that they *are* twelve-foot lizards is that none of them has ever tried to sue him for saying it.

Now, this got me to thinking. How brilliant would it be if the Queen sued David Icke and had to *prove* in a court of law that she wasn't a lizard? Who wouldn't want to watch that?

And that's why it is my contention that we are indeed being ruled by a global élite of shape-shifting lizards. Purely because I would like to see how somebody would prove that they are not.

In fact, along with the Queen and George Bush the following people are also all *definitely* shape-shifting lizards:

**DAVID HASSELHOFF**

**YOUR MUM**

**CHRIS MARTIN OUT OF COLDPLAY**

**XANDER**

I will gladly see all of you enormous lizards in Kettering
Crown Court.

# 20

# SHOULD WE HAVE A THIRD BABY?

You'll never regret having a baby. Never ever ever. Not in the long run. And not just because, in the long run, you might have the pleasure of watching *them* suffer the pains of parenthood. But because, however grim the grim bits are and – let's be quite clear – there are times when you will be *literally* certifiable with sleeplessness, anxiety, and gibbering, grunting fury, you will come out of it with a little person who says 'wowij' instead of 'sausage' and at the sight of whose hot, sleeping form you will make that face where your chin goes all dimply. So, yes, apart from the fleeting, entirely human moments of wishing the little bugger was miles away ruining his grandparents' evening instead, you'll never regret having a baby. But the question that viewer Sam Mould and his wife wanted us to answer is: *should* they have a third baby, and that is a very different consideration.

One of the good things about babies is that you do at least

get a few months' warning. I mean, imagine if you didn't:

'Darling, I'm pregnant, I'm having a baby.'

'When?'

'Now.'

'Oh, brilliant . . . Oh, hang on, let me just roll up the new carpet.'

All the same, as the Moulds will testify, it is a massive adjustment to go from having no babies* to having one baby.** (Last year, on a slightly separate issue, we went from having no llamas to having two llamas. I know, *two*. But, then, who hasn't fallen for those honeyed words 'Buy One Get One Free'? On the 'Having Some Llamas' scale I can tell you we really hit the ground running – and llamas don't even need burping.*** All they have in common with human offspring is that they like spitting and they have a knack of looking superior, even when they actually know sod all.) But the temptation is to assume that, having made the big step up to having children at all, the addition of more little Moulds will just get easier and easier – after all, you've got the kit.

..................................................................................

* Really quite easy.
** Quite hard.
*** God, at least I hope they don't.

Well, yes, if you're cooking three fish fingers it's no hardship to cook six instead, but it *is* twice as many ketchup hand-prints to wash off the wall, twice as many noses to blow, and it reduces by precisely half the already slim chance of a decent night's sleep. On the plus side, it increases your chance of doing something you've not done since you were yourself a kid: eating a fish finger. Even if it's a leftover fish finger. You'd never cook it yourself, but there it is, in all its squidgy, orangy, breadcrumby, vaguely fishy glory. Mm. God, I'm *so* glad we had kids.

But three?

Here's a handy checklist for you to consider before arriving at your answer.

Are you happy being the kind of person you'd far, far rather hate, driving a stupid big car from now on because they're the only ones that'll fit all those car seats in? Would you really be happy in this car? One more baby will do a lot of things to you, but most importantly, it will put off even further your purchase of the mid-life-crisis Ferrari. Still happy?

Are you planning to embark on any kind of showbiz family-type career in which three children are going to be key (for forming bicycling pyramids, providing backing vocals, or even just minding the queue while you and Mrs Mould get into your leopard skin)?

Do you accept that even the best possible seating arrangement on a train or ski-lift would leave one of you sitting on their own? (If you answer, 'That's absolutely fine, if it's me', you really have had enough kids already.)

Are you ready to accept that every game they play together will always leave one of them being ball-boy/ drinks superintendent/person who screams, 'Mummy, they're not letting me play.' In other words, are you happy to follow the words 'Go out and play together' with, inside two minutes, 'Yes, all right, I'm coming. I really wasn't relaxing with that novel/glass of wine/ novel and glass of wine at all'?

Are you comfortable with the fact that from here on in you will be outnumbered by your children and that there will come a time when they will join forces to GET THEIR WAY?

Mull over all of these and if you answer 'no' to any of— You know what? Have a third baby. Go right for it. Put this book down and get on with 'having that baby'. Put the other two in front of *Peppa Pig*\*\*\*\* and tiptoe upstairs. Go on,

...................................................................................

\*\*\*\* Put it on *Peppa* shuffle – that'll go on for hours. Have you got the one with Captain Daddy Dog in it? That's the best one they've ever made. Who *is* that actor? He's brilliant.

what are you waiting for? Or are you both just too bloody tired?

When you're having this discussion about a fourth, though, get each of your three children to bang a drum while you read through the handy checklist above.

# 19
# WHICH IS THE BEST CRISP FLAVOUR?

If you read our first book *The 100 Most Pointless Things in the World* then you are a terrific human being. And that's not simply my opinion, that's an actual scientific fact.

But you will also be aware that I have *very* strong opinions on crisps. Particularly ready-salted crisps.

The only things I really, really, really care about in this world are war, poverty, injustice, oppression, my children, Fulham FC and crisps. And chocolate.*

..................................................................................................

* I do also care about what your brother-in-law said during Christmas dinner. I can't believe he said that. What is his problem? Are you OK? Let's just open this bottle of wine and forget all about him. He's Sally's problem.

So when I ask the question 'Which is the best crisp flavour?'
I don't ask it lightly. And, also, I already know the answer.
It is absolutely indisputable. You know it too if you're honest.

So, if you think one of the following is the best crisp flavour
you're wrong:

CHEESE AND ONION

PRAWN COCKTAIL

BARBECUE BEEF

WORCESTER SAUCE

ROAST CHICKEN

SOME RIDICULOUS THING WITH GROUND
ECUADORIAN PEPPER AND CARAWAY SEEDS

SMOKY BACON

JALAPEÑO

OX

BISON

WOLF

DOLPHIN

CHUTNEY AND CHEDDAR

CHEDDAR AND CHUTNEY

MATURE CHEDDAR AND SPICY CHUTNEY

SPICY CHEDDAR AND MATURE CHUTNEY

ANYTHING ADVERTISED BY TARA PALMER-
TOMKINSON

HORSE

HORSE AND ONION

KETCHUP

STEAK

STRAWBERRY

STRAWBERRY CARAMEL SWIRL

CHOCOLATE CHUNK CHIP

I RAN OUT OF REAL FLAVOURS SOME TIME AGO

EGG AND CRESS

UM . . . COMPUTER?

DESK?

BOOK

DEADLINE

READY SALTED

And if you think the following is the best crisp flavour, you're right:

**SALT AND VINEGAR**

Let's move on.

## POINTLESS FACTS

Gary Lineker and Michael Owen are both from Leicester, Gary is the face of Walker's Crisps. He was quite happy to endorse 'Salt and Lineker' crisps, and Michael Owen agreed to 'Cheese and Owen'; but a certain superstar wouldn't play ball with 'Smoky Beckham'.

# 18
# HOW LONG AFTER A DATE SHOULD YOU TEXT SOMEONE?

How long after? The next day. That's it. The very next day.
What time? 11 a.m., on the dot. Not too eager, not too rude.
Indeed if, as you hit 'send', you find a similar text just
arriving, you'll realise that both of you have read *this* book.
And if you *have* both read this book, then congratulations!
There is no more secure foundation for a loving relationship
than sharing the same immaculate good taste. But if you
both love *Pointless*, your pairing is truly blessed, your love
will bloom and your relationship will go from strength to
strength, right up to the moment your 'soul mate' tearfully
reveals that this book was, in fact, an unwanted Christmas
present.

As for the text of the text, the 11 a.m. text doesn't have to
be effusive: it just has to say (a) something nice, like 'I checked
out that Justin Bieber album – you're right he *is* amazing,'

and (b) 'That was a fun night.'* And it's (b) that's the important bit. Even if it wasn't. Even if you spent three hours the previous night sitting there wondering how you could ever have misjudged it so badly, you've got to say something. And saying nothing will just make it all the more incredibly awkward. Awkward for both of you, as you re-enact one of the terrible silences of the night before, only on a fresh media platform. You should at least make the 'text part' of the date work, with a cleaner break than last night's 'Well . . . right . . . erm . . . we . . . we must, er . . . yup, 'bye. 'Bye. 'Bye.' After all, you'd never text *that*, would you?

'Silence is golden' – so sang the Tremeloes in their number-one hit of 1967. But they were wrong. Silence is awful. Silence is the worst. Even the best evenings in the world can be pulled apart in the mind, and seeing as there were only two of you there, if one corroborator doesn't chip in with something it can all start to turn a bit Grand Guignol in the other's

....................................................................................

* Even this harmless-seeming message is a bit tricky. 'That was a fun night' could sound very sarcastic, especially if preceded in the reader's head by a silent 'Well . . .' Perhaps it's safer to go with a straight 'That was fun.' Or could that be read as dripping with irony too? Would it help to add an exclamation mark? No, that's not cool, that's saying, 'Look, a joke!' In fact, when it comes to irony in printed form, we're entering a whole new area. A minefield so fraught with potential disaster that it may need another entire chapter to itself. Or another book.

memory. So, send that text. It may be a chore, but doing the decent thing usually is. The chore bit is half of what makes it so damned decent.

The only possible reason for not texting at 11 a.m. would be that you are so madly keen on the previous evening's date that you don't want to appear too keen in case it might somehow put them off. But no, take it from your *Pointless* chums, that just starts to look like tricksy game-playing and risks making you look like a nutjob. The rule is: text the next day. At 11**.

......................................................................

** Of course, this advice really just concerns the earlier points in the dating timeline. Naturally, if the dating is repeated . . . and repeated . . . and soon you're at it like knives . . . and texting sixty seconds after parting, with a lewd *double-entendre* that only the two of you will 'get', then the rules will change and keep changing. That's the nature of relationships: the rules keep changing. However long you're together, the rules keep bloody changing . . . from that first date and that follow-up text, to the moment you call it a day or, if all goes really well, one of you dies.

# 17

# ARE WE GOING TO LET RICHARD'S GEEKY WORDPLAY QUIZZES RUIN OUR CHRISTMAS AGAIN? (PART 2)

How did you get on with the UK cities quiz? Mum got a nosebleed and Karen put Steve in hospital with a single punch? Excellent.

Here's another for you, thirty clues, anagrams, bad puns, infuriating wordplay, the usual. This time, though, all of the clues have a Christmas theme because I know you bought this book at Christmas. And if you didn't buy this book at Christmas then you probably got it a lot cheaper, and you should be grateful that you're getting a quiz at all.

All the answers to the clues below are Capital Cities of the World. Again, I would print out a list, as there are a few obscure ones here. Good luck, and don't forget to avoid eye-contact with Karen at all times.

1. I Go Santa Crazy!
2. More Like A Christmas Nut
3. The French Like The Queen's Speech
4. Cliff Richard Rubbish
5. What's Missing From 'Santa's Rindr'
6. Where I Get These Terrible Christmas Puns From

The next six questions are my Christmas present list.

7. Reserve A Spa Day  (Mum)
8. Stairlift (Nan)
9. 2010 Ryder Cup Film (Brother)
10. Otis Redding Album (Sister)
11. Personal Car Cleaner (Uncle)
12. Something Else (For Someone ELSE)

And the next six relate to Christmas dinner.

13. Place For Turkey Juices
14. Lamb? Nope! Ridiculous!
15. We're Getting Our Christmas Food Somewhere
    Different This Year
16. Overcook The Roast Potatoes
17. Outlaw Chicken
18. Not Whiting, But Not Browning Either

And the rest are just annoying and difficult again.

19. Father Christmas's Third, Fourth And Fifth
20. Chrimbo Got A Clue Inside
21. Balthazar's One Hundred
22. I Stop Three Ships Come Sailing In. Who Am I?
23. Boy, Nazareth
24. Six French Hens, Four Turtle Doves And Two
    Partridges In Two Pear Trees
25. Sounds Like Joseph. Or Jesus. Or Me.
26. Looks Like Joseph. Or Jesus. Or Me.
27. Scariest Cracker
28. Back-Up Wrapping Paper And Eggnog
29. Involved In So Dismal A Boxing Day
30. Jeered A Grinch

# 16

# SHOULD YOU CORRECT SOMEONE WHO KEEPS CALLING YOU BY THE WRONG NAME?

Who knows what flies through our parents' heads when they come to choose by what noise we will be known for the rest of our lives? If you're Gwyneth Paltrow, mother of Moses and Apple, it'll depend on which bit of the Bible you're reading, or the make of tablet you're reading it on. If you're David Beckham, it's more a question of 'What do I want tattooed on my left buttock?' But however it arrives, eventually they stumble across that perfect combination of clicks, grunts and plosives that they feel best captures our as yet unidentifiable identities, it is duly entered on our birth certificate, and over time we learn to inhabit that noise and make it our own. Some of the noises can be nice and short – here I'm thinking of noises along the lines of 'Dave', 'Will', 'Mark' or 'Kwok'. Others can be rather longer, more a string of noises – and here I'm specifically thinking of 'Alexander'. Leaving aside for the moment that a large portion of the populace chooses not to recognise the difference between 'Alexander' and 'Alexandra' (which is a girl's name) and will, for example, happily write 'Alexandra' down on a guest pass for someone who is (a) standing in front of them, (b) quite clearly male, and (c) going to have to wear it for the rest of the day in front of everyone like a great big girl, I want to focus on the kind of challenge the name 'Alexander' evidently presents to people.

There is another name, 'Alastair', which is not very like 'Alexander' at all. It is one whole syllable shorter; to mistake 'Alastair' for 'Alexander' would be like mistaking Ronnie Corbett for Richard Osman. But they both start with 'Al' and end with 'er' and that, for many, is good enough. This is owing to a far-from-uncommon sensory blind spot in the brain to which scientists have given the technical term 'laziness'. And so to many people I am called Alastair: 'Alastair,' they will say, expecting me to turn and give them my ear. This is not a daily occurrence but more probably a weekly one. Let's say every fortieth person who talks to me calls me Alastair. Alexander the Great went through much the same, which is why one in every fortieth person who talked to *him* was, more often than not, disembowelled.

The problem is, 'Alastair' is not my name. 'Alastair' is not the sound I have been trained to respond to. Trying to get my attention by calling 'Alastair!' across the room is as useful as blowing a dog-whistle to get the cat in. It would be grossly unjust to genuine Alastairs present (and I like the majority of those I've met)* if I started tuning in to their noise and turning round to say, 'Yes?' And I don't want to run the risk of appearing rude. So I make it a point of principle always to correct someone the minute they get my name wrong, even if I have to do it fifteen times.

---

* This is far easier to say if you've never met Alastair Campbell.

# 15
## WHAT IS THE BEST SUPERPOWER TO HAVE?

I don't know if you ever watch *Question Time*, but sometimes I feel they have their priorities wrong. I do *know*, of course, that rail privatisation and Scottish devolution are important. And I *am* interested to hear what the Lib Dem Agriculture and Fisheries spokesman and someone who used to be in a Britpop band think of both issues. But imagine this for a moment.

**DIMBLEBY**

Our next question is from a Mr Alan Jenkinson of Dundee. Mr Jenkinson?

**MR JENKINSON**

In light of how bored I am by all the other questions this evening, particularly the one about quantitative easing, I wonder what the panel believe would be the best superpower to have?

**DIMBLEBY**

So, the best superpower to have? Theresa May?

Now we'd have a proper debate. No name-calling, back-covering, grandstanding or scapegoating. But what would the panel conclude?

This is truly one of the toughest arguments to solve in the whole book. Working out if God is real was an absolute breeze compared to working out the best superpower to have. Let's start by narrowing it down to a top five.

Invisibility
Flight
Teleportation
Mind-reading
Time-freeze

Ask everyone around your Christmas dinner table to choose the best of these. I guarantee the debate will last long into the afternoon. I also guarantee that your Uncle Tony will immediately say, 'Invisibility,' and will not change his mind at any point. That's Uncle Tony for you.

Let's take them one by one.

*Invisibility.* Brilliant obviously, and not just for the reasons that Uncle Tony thinks it's brilliant. You could go anywhere, get in free anywhere, travel on any private jet, walk into any bank vault. But let's stop and think for a second. Yes, you could stow aboard first-class on any plane in the world, but every time you switched on an in-flight movie the steward would switch it off, so you could only watch *Madagascar 3* in fifteen-second bursts. You could sneak into a bank vault, but you couldn't steal anything: you're invisible but that doesn't suddenly make gold invisible. And I can't help thinking that most of the benefits of invisibility are covered in better ways by teleportation and time-freeze. Invisibility is out.

*Flight.* The worst of all, surely. It would be *fun* to fly, but it's fun to go ten-pin bowling, and that's not a superpower. It would also be tiring. Like air-running. You know when you can't be bothered to go to the gym? Being able to fly would be like that every day.

*Teleportation.* OK, now we're at the business end of this argument. Teleportation allows us to go anywhere in the world at a moment's notice. Holiday, Cup Final, home from work. We could teleport into a bank vault, then back out again with the gold (beat that, Invisibility). So, in fact, we wouldn't have to go to work. Teleportation would be particularly useful when you're at the end of your Tesco shop and you realise you forgot something from the first aisle. Like if, for some reason, you wanted a cauliflower. Teleportation is a contender.

*Mind-reading.* This one starts out by sounding brilliant, but gets worse and worse the more you think about it. The plus side is, of course, that you know what everyone is thinking at all times. The downside is, of course, that *you know what everyone is thinking at all times.* I mean, my God, can you begin to *imagine* it? Think of how bored you get just listening to what people around you *say* all day, and then think of the appalling rubbish they're actually *thinking*! The stuff they say is actually the edited highlights (what Ant and Dec would call their 'best bits'). It would be beyond awful. And you'd also find out what people actually think of you, which I promise you wouldn't want to know. For example, that new receptionist doesn't actually fancy you. That look she gives you is just her thinking, That reminds me, I must ring Dad.

*Time-freeze.* Interesting. The ability to walk unencumbered through the world as everything is stopped, motionless, around you. The potential for mischief and larceny is almost mind-blowing. Even Uncle Tony could surely see the benefits. I think it beats invisibility because it essentially *is* invisibility, but without the attendant downsides (i.e. inability to watch *Madagascar* unencumbered on aeroplanes). But it feels maybe that time-freeze is only for the deviants and criminals among us, and we all like to pretend that we're not deviants and criminals. Which was why your parents told you Uncle Tony went on that two-year holiday a few years ago.

So, whatever you've concluded around your Christmas dinner table – still squabbling as the Queen struggled to be heard over your dad saying, 'No, no, no, but you don't understand. Flying would be *cool*' – there is only one conclusion here.

The best superpower is *teleportation*. And if you disagree, then the next time you get up to go to the loo, I want you to remember that you wouldn't have to get up to go to the loo if you could teleport.

# 14

# TEA? SUPPER? DINNER? CAN WE JUST SORT THIS OUT ONCE AND FOR ALL?

It's high time we all decided what we're going to call our evening meal. Dinner? Is that what you want? Dinner? OK, fine we'll call it dinner.

Much as this will disappoint traditionalists, who feel dinner is a formal affair, it can't be denied that there is such a thing as 'common usage'. For instance, everyone who uses the word 'karaoke' naturally pronounces it 'carry-oakie' and if you say, 'No, it should be "kara", as in the Japanese word for "empty", the whole word meaning "empty orchestra",' you will simply be mocked for your pedantry and punched in the face to the sound of 'Total Eclipse Of The Heart'. The fact is: every language evolves and English is no exception.

But traditionalists don't surrender their traditions easily – it's always been that way. Hang on, they cry, isn't dinner quite a special thing? Hence having its own starchy dress code and of course the 'dinner party'? Where else do you get the chance to sit down and eat with people you don't know or like and have stilted conversations about how you know the host, and where your children should be educated? All right, maybe there are also tea parties and supper parties, but I'm pretty sure I've never seen anyone in a tea jacket.* And that's the point, isn't it? That's why supper's called 'supper' so you know it's not dinner (no need to dress up, no danger of any kind of seafood starter in a glass) and that it's OK to eat it in front of the telly. And then there's tea, which covers every-thing from toast and jam with a mug of tea some time around five-ish, watching *Pointless*, to a hot evening meal (sometimes also with a mug of tea) any time before *The One Show*.

So this is a right old dog's dinner/tea/supper. Not that dogs have this problem. For them, no meal requires a name, just a full bowl. But, for the sake of humanity, let's try to impose some order here. Shall we say that 'tea' is anything before six? Everyone happy with that? 'Dinner' is a more formal evening meal, and 'supper' a more casual one? What's wrong with that? Couple of people shaking their heads. It seems everyone now calls it 'dinner', 'tea' is just a drink, and 'supper' is only for prime ministers and their inner circle (in contrast to 'Dinner with the Prime Minister', which is open to anyone willing to bung a few grand in his campaign pot). Oh, God,

........................................................................

* Unless it's the kind of quilted thing favoured by our queen and certain drug-dealers.

and now I've just remembered 'high tea'. Where are we going to put that?

OK, OK, for this one I'm going to say just call it what you've always been comfortable calling it. It's one of those arguments where instead of resolution we'll just have to enjoy the variety of differing opinions. After all, at heart, a meal is just like any other meeting. The key thing is for all concerned to know the time and the place. Get those two bits sorted, the rest will follow and no one will go hungry. You have your rules, I have mine. If a mutual acquaintance invites us to his home for tea at six and you hear 'dinner' and I hear 'supper', then what's the problem? You'll turn up in black tie, I'll turn up in my comfiest, baggiest, holeyest jumper and we can get to know each other over a cup of Earl Grey and a Hobnob. Even better, we'll now have something to talk about.

# 13
## WHY ARE YOU BEING SO DEFENSIVE?

'Why are you being so defensive?' is the single most annoying thing that anyone can *ever* say during an argument.

This is mainly because of the logic bomb that makes 'I'm *not* being defensive' an impossible reply.

Also, though, if you actually *are* being defensive, you are usually at such a crucial stage of the argument that it's really not the time to show any weakness.

So is there any answer you can give to 'Why are you being so defensive?'

There is now.

The second the words have been uttered, simply take this book off the shelf and point to the following:

HI, STEVE/JULIE (delete as applicable).

If you are reading this, it means that you have just uttered the words 'why are you being so defensive?' during an argument. I don't know what the argument is about; I'm assuming it's the bins.

We both understand that there is no answer to 'why are you being so defensive?'

We also both understand that we love each other.

We further understand that it's good to have an argument every now and again, but they never really last.

So, strictly speaking we could both just agree to end this one right now and go to the pub? Or we could watch that new Danish crime thing on BBC4? It's supposed to be really good once you get into it. What do you reckon?

I'll give you a couple of minutes to think about it while I take the bins out.

Lots of love

Julie/Steve (delete as applicable)

# 12

# FICTIONAL ADDRESSES –
# DO WE CARE WHERE OUR
# CHARACTERS LIVE?

My life at home is the same as my life at work. Pointless. I spend a colossal proportion of my life at fictional addresses. This is not a tax wheeze (as far as I understand), just something I like to do on a quiet day, just me, a dark room and Primelocation up on the screen. But books are strewn with actual fictional addresses: details of flats and houses where their protagonists live. Occasionally they are completely made up but appended with just enough features for us to be able to place them in our own limited geographies; other times they are specific locations where future generations will be able to open themed cafés and gift shops (where everything for sale is complete tat, with the possible exception of the book that's to blame for it all) and current inhabitants can experience a spike in property prices, longer queues at the deli counter, and busloads of tourists taking photos of *their* house by mistake. Or maybe *not* by mistake, if someone's left the window open while they shower.

Below is a little test to see how much you really remember about characters' addresses. Who lives at these houses? To make it easier their initials are in brackets.

## POINTLESS QUIZ

1. 62 West Wallaby Street, Wigan, Lancs (G)
2. 124 Conch Street, Bikini Bottom, Pacific Ocean (SS)
3. 4 Privet Drive, Little Whinging, Surrey (HP)
4. 13 Coronation Street, Weatherfield, G. Manchester (HO)
5. Danemead, St Mary Mead (JM)
6. 7 Eccles Street, Dublin, Ireland (LB)
7. Apt 1901, Eliot Bay Towers, Seattle, Washington (FC)
8. 742 Evergreen Terrace, Springfield, USA (HS)
9. Pemberley, Derbyshire, UK (FD)
10. 32 Windsor Gardens, Notting Hill, London (PB)
11. 221B Baker Street, London, UK (SH)
12. 1630 Revello Drive, Sunnydale, CA (BS)

# 11 DO I PLAY TOO MANY VIDEO GAMES?

Below is a series of questions with yes/no answers. If you answer mainly 'yes', you play too many video games. If you answer mainly 'no', you're fine for now. If you're not reading this because you're playing World of Warcraft, we both already know the answer.

1. Have you ever missed an important meeting because you were searching for a magic sword in an enchanted forest?
2. Have you ever gone ten-pin bowling and been incredulous that you can't get as many strikes as you can on the Wii?
3. Is the only wildlife you saw last week Sonic the Hedgehog?
4. Have you and Josh from school ever wiped out an entire Iraqi army platoon before breakfast?
5. At a family funeral of a close and much-loved relative,

have you ever looked at the coffin and mentally flipped it lengthways to make it easier to use in Tetris?

6. Have you ever considered calling your children Mario and Zelda? Or Bowser?

7. While sitting in a traffic jam have you ever secretly wished that your life was more like Grand Theft Auto?

8. Does the 'qualifications' section of your CV mention 'Angry Birds'?

9. Were you surprised to discover they had made a book of the Harry Potter video games?

10. Have you *ever* said, 'Daaaaad! I just need to finish this stage'?

How did you do? While you're totting up your scores could I make just one more observation about video games?

When I was young I would do almost anything to get a day off school. My mum would head off to work and I would be left alone in the house. It would take me about half an hour to remember that I didn't *really* have a sore throat and therefore could get up and plan a whole day of non-stop entertainment.

Here were my options.

1. Feel Smug For Forty-Five Minutes
2. Sit Around For Hours With Literally Nothing To Do
3. Watch *Pebble Mill At One*

4. Have Potato Waffles For Lunch
5. Worry That If I Get Any More Bored I Might Actually Have To Read A Book Of All Things
6. Wait For Children's TV To Start At Three, By Which Time My Friends Were Getting Out Of School Anyway

If my son wants a day off school these are his options:

1. Slaughter Zombies
2. Win The Monaco Grand Prix
3. Drive Around An Imaginary New York Killing Drug-dealers
4. Have Potato Waffles For Lunch
5. Play A Round At St Andrews Against Tiger Woods
6. Pull Off A Bank Heist With Two Indonesian Brothers And A Canadian Goth

So why is *anybody* going to school any more?

# 10
# SHOULD WE LIKE FRENCH PEOPLE?

Tread anywhere in the British Isles and it's impossible not to feel a strong sense of kindred spirit – quite possibly one you'd happily disown the moment someone tries to sell you life insurance or overtake you before the next bend, but one you can see quite plainly. Then look across the continent to our cousins the Germans and their neighbours the Poles, and theirs, the Belarussians and beyond, and there it still is, a personality and body shape that we all have some part of, forged by years of terrible weather and worse diet. We're a fleshy bunch, fond of beer and a variety of sausages, with a tendency towards bottling up our tempers and losing our hair. We resent too much, we exercise too little, and we wear clothes whose shapes and functions are as ancient as their textiles are modern. We shout at each other, we even fight each other, but at the end of the day we are brother and sister, despite our many differences, thanks to the geography we share.

Actually, hang on, that can't be right. Because look who lives right next door to us, closer, in fact, to our capital than most of the rest of the country. Look at them, all rangy and sexy and exotic. No, not the Welsh – look the other way. Yes, I'm talking about the French. Instead of our flabby Saxon pallor, they have a dark demeanour and a peculiar constellation of exquisitely chiselled features, evolved over centuries for the optimum expression of haughty indifference. It's a wonder William the Conqueror even *bothered* to invade in 1066. I mean, how indifferent can you be about a battle that you report back not via messenger on horseback or sealed scroll, but several years' worth of needlework? They even grow at a different rate from us – see how they remain children right up until their eighteenth birthdays and then suddenly – *sacrebleu*\* – they emerge as forthright, sophisticated Frenchies. Where we tut and scowl and store up a generation of griev-ances over imagined slights and next-door's leylandii, the French rise to instant rancour, hitting one another, if neces-sary with livestock,\*\* before sitting down the best of friends to share a (small) glass of wine. They can't do pop music for love or money,\*\*\* but they make excellent films with subtitles

........................................................................................

\* This is a French curse, which can be literally translated as 'sacred blue', in derogatory reference to Margaret Thatcher.

\*\* I have seen this. With a sheep. I promise.

\*\*\* The only possible exception is 'Je T'Aime (Moi Non Plus)', though this is not really a pop song so much as the soundtrack of a porn movie that, following a mix-up, was accidentally recorded

during which you will invariably see someone's pubic hair. They flounce, they pout, they dress with improbable feminine flair and discuss existentialism without fear of being glassed in the face. They are, in short, our nemesis.

Should we try to emulate the French? Of course we should: all of our best attributes were nicked from them at one time or another. Should we get on with the French? Again, the answer is yes: they are – however improbably – our neighbours, or what David Walliams would call 'within easy swimming distance', and that will never change so *entente* is helpful. But should we like the French? Absolutely not.

..............................

on vinyl. As a result, there is, somewhere, a French porno where the girl reaches a climax to the sound of a long-forgotten Warrington skiffle band.

# WHO IS THE BEST DR WHO?

This is a question that is incredibly fiercely argued in certain circles. You know the type of circles I'm talking about. Live and let live is what I say.

But, despite the endless arguments, the answer is actually simple.

# The best Doctor Who is whoever the Doctor was when you were eleven.

# Or David Tennant.

# 8

# WITNESS SIGNATURES – ARE THEY WORTH THE PAPER THEY'RE WRITTEN ON?

Car keys? Yup, got 'em. Er . . . Mum's birthday card? Yup, just . . . finishing . . . that . . . now . . . Yup, done. With three kisses. Or did I send her five last year? Will she notice? Of course she bloody will. Five kisses, why not? Be generous, it's her birthday! What else? Phone? Where the hell is it? Who's nicked my bloody—? Oh, it's in my pocket. Anything else? Oh, yes, there's that form I've got to sign. I'll just do that now and I can pop it in the . . . What's this? A witness signature? Witness? What? Who? Why? Aaaaargh.

And so the document stays on the side in the kitchen for weeks stretching into months, operating as an occasional coaster for your coffee mug, with a couple of hastily scribbled phone numbers on the back, plus the words 'tea bags, loo rolls, milk', until a reminder comes through requesting its urgent return. So now, for a few days, you have *two* coasters and jotting pads, but inevitably the moment comes when a 'new you' decides to get a grip. Right, here we go! So . . . who shall we ask to do it? Unless . . . Hmm . . .

Should one of you maybe just pretend to be someone else and then it can get sent off? It's the most obvious solution by a million miles. It's also, according to the block capitals at the foot of the page, A CRIME. A crime? Most crimes need a witness, but to commit a crime by *pretending* to be a witness? What kind of Kafkaesque nightmare are you about to sign up for – or, rather, *not* sign up for, by signing up as someone else? So, instead, the form travels into work with you in your bag – you'll get someone at the office to witness your signature. Easy. But no matter how dull or tedious things get at work, nothing feels as dull or tedious as the thought of digging out that form and asking Sandra from Accounts if she could spare a couple of minutes to do something really dull and tedious. So the form remains at the bottom of your bag until it's become one with all the other bits of paper at the bottom of your bag, forming a geological layer with directions to the wedding of a friend who's long since divorced, a Christmas shopping list from when your children still wanted Lego, and the first of the urgent reminders they sent you . . .

Some witnesses are specifically required to be 'upstanding members of the community', which means company directors, JPs, doctors,* vicars or daytime game-show hosts; others are

---

* What makes a doctor's signature so authoritative? There are

not specified so presumably they could be literally anyone from Van Morrison to the guy with the stocking on his head who's running out of the Abbey National on the corner.** What, though, is the point? What possible extra heft is brought to my form by dint of its having the Revd Dr Julia Goodhead JP's signature appended to it (yes, all right, one of us did pretend to be someone else) rather than just my own? I have absolutely no idea.

Are witness signatures worth the paper they're written on? No, they're not. So, if you want to go to Downing Street with a petition demanding that the whole system be abolished, I'll happily sign it. With 500 different names.

........................

people in the UK right now whose passport photos will have been witnessed by Harold Shipman. Not that I'm implying he was untruthful in those instances. I'd hate to tarnish his reputation further. But all the same . . .

** Although it's not Abbey National any more, it's Santander. Not even your bank has a consistent identity and still your signature needs to be witnessed???

# IS IT EVER OKAY TO WALK OUT BEFORE THE END OF A FILM?

Hmm. This is an unusual one. The answer seems blindingly obvious. If you're in the cinema, sitting through a painfully unfunny comedy, or a painfully *funny* psychological drama, or maybe a Jennifer Aniston film, the most natural thing in the world would be to get up, walk out, and spend your evening doing something more fun. For example, the sink in the bathroom needs unblocking.

I think perhaps I have something approaching an answer. Let's say we're pretty sure the film is terrible after about twenty minutes. We're thoughtful and compassionate people, so we naturally give it another twenty minutes or so, just to make sure. By this point we are now forty minutes through and we come to a realisation: we have just completely wasted forty minutes of our life. If we leave now we are throwing away those forty minutes for ever. But, and here's the crux, if we stay, we probably only have about another forty minutes to go (those Jennifer Aniston films tend not to be three hours long) and at least at the end of it we will have an anecdote about a terrible film we've sat through, and we won't have to unblock the sink.

And also we might be on a date, and that's an impossible position to be in. You keep stealing glances at your companion, trying to read her expression. Is she bored or enthralled? If you lean over and say, 'Shall we go?' will she look aghast and whisper, 'Are you crazy? This is some of the finest Eastern European cinematography I have ever seen!' In which case, for the sake of politeness, you're going to have to sit through the whole of the rest of the film, and she's still not going to sleep with you. I bet you wish you hadn't finished your pick 'n' mix now.

But our job here is to solve arguments, and on this occasion I think I have to conclude that it *is* OK to leave a film before the end. I know it's difficult, and I'm not encouraging it, but if you ever feel the urge becomes too strong, or you get a definite visual signal that your date is yawning or looking for opportunities to self-harm, please feel free to leave. You know what happens in the end anyway: Jennifer Aniston marries the nice guy she would never actually marry in real life.

Now that that's successfully dealt with, how about some more quiz questions? I'm going to give you twelve famous last lines of films, all of which you would have missed if you'd walked out. Can you get a lower score than the rest of your family (most of whom fall asleep before the end of films, as you know)?

## POINTLESS QUIZ

1. 'Roads? Where we're going we don't need roads' (1985)
2. 'All right, Mr DeMille. I'm ready for my close-up' (1950)
3. 'There's no place like home' (1939)
4. 'And he would be there when Jem waked up in the morning' (1962)
5. 'Kevin, what did you do to my room?' (1990)
6. 'Why, she wouldn't even harm a fly' (1960)
7. 'After all, tomorrow is another day' (1939)
8. 'Well, nobody's perfect' (1959)
9. 'Hello, everybody. This is Mrs Norman Maine' (1937)
10. 'Love means never having to say you're sorry' (1970)
11. 'It was Beauty killed the Beast' (1933)
12. 'Hang on, lads, I've got a great idea' (1969)

# 6

# DO I REALLY NEED TO KNOW WHO, SAY, NICKI MINAJ IS?

It used to be you could only get famous in this country for displaying some kind of inherent talent or ability. Like singing, playing cricket or Victorian serial-killing. But, these days, the lines of celebrity have become blurred. Now you can become a household name by simply being rich – I'm looking at you, Paris Hilton – find fame through doing whatever it is that Kerry Katona does, or even bag a *Sun* front page for chucking someone's cat into a bin in Coventry. Paris Hilton again, I think.

But do you really need to know who famous people are? I have chosen Nicki Minaj* to represent them all. Never heard of Nicki Minaj? Let's find out if that's acceptable.

...........................................................................

\* Nicki Minaj was 2008 World Superbike Champion, and is currently shadow defence secretary.

I am now in my forties and have been learning who famous people are since about 1975. Mike Yarwood was probably the first. Unless Basil Brush counts.

The trouble is, though, your mental Rolodex of celeb names very soon becomes a one-in-one-out scenario, and I'm worried that my efforts to try to remember who or what a Nicki Minaj is, may force me to forget Sir Edmund Hillary, Glenys Kinnock or six-times World Snooker Champion Ray Reardon. And I'd like to see Nicki Minaj conquer Everest or attempt a difficult red along the cushion, especially under the bright lights of the Crucible.

It's all because people who used to be famous are *still famous*, and now new ones are being added all the time. So Keith Harris is still famous, but now Danny off *The Voice* is too. Lulu is still famous but so is Paul Hollywood from *The Great British Bake Off*. It all turns into an enormous celebrity mountain. The sort of mountain that could only be climbed by, um, that guy, the old mountaineer who climbed Everest. You know, thingy.

So, for example, I am perfectly capable of naming all five members of One Direction, but I have recently realised that I have forgotten the entire Southampton midfield who won the 1976 FA Cup final (Peter Something was one of them). The sheer number, similarity and density of famous people has become baffling. So, should we even try to keep up?

Well, the truth is, certain celebrity conversations are unavoidable. Whether in the pub, at the hairdresser's, or with your grandsons. So to help you, here's a handy cut-out-and-keep guide to 'the only famous people you need to know the name of to get by in modern Britain'.

1. The England manager – currently Uncle Roy Hodgson. Example of use: 'What was Hodgson playing at against Lithuania?'

2. One person from *Corrie* and one from *EastEnders* – so when you turn it on after a six-month absence to exclaim, 'I don't know who any of these people are', a familiar face will eventually pop up on screen. I call this the 'Ian Beale Principle'.

3. One National Treasure. There is always someone whom *everybody* agrees is awesome at any given time. It's usually Victoria Wood, though sometimes it can be Stephen Fry or Miranda Hart or, if you want to be very cool, Olivia Colman. Example of use: 'Isn't Claire Balding just wonderful?'

4. Someone modern. Just pick one at random. How about Ed Sheeran? Don't worry about who he actually is, and don't be afraid to drop his name into conversation liberally. Example of use: 'I know you think I'm out of touch, but even *I* know who Ed Sheeran is. And I also know who Rizzle Kicks is.'

5. Phillip Schofield. By all means feel free to know more than just these people, but the above is a bare

minimum. If you promise me faithfully that you will stick by those rules then you have my absolute permission not to know who Nicki Minaj is. And if you don't want to know then don't look at the answer at the bottom of the page.

In closing, here are three people I've picked at random from the *Mail Online* website today: Cara Delevingne, Kendall Jenner and Jamie Laing. I don't know who any of them are. Which means, for the moment, I can still remember the cast of *Rentaghost*.

# 5

# SHOULD YOU LEAVE THE LOO SEAT UP OR DOWN?

Another of the all-time classic domestic arguments. In fact, now I really think about it, there have been an awful lot of toilet-based arguments in this book. What is it about the toilet that's driving us mad? If anything, the toilet should be furious with *us*.

The answer to this one is actually fairly easy, but to reach it we're going to have to get a bit technical. Are we all happy to get technical about our toilet habits?

The basic issue is that no one really wants to be handling the loo seat, whether to prop it up or to pop it back down. So our quest is to discover how we minimise this.

To solve this argument once and for all, let us imagine a scenario. Don't panic, you won't have to imagine it *too* closely.

We have one toilet shared by one man and one woman. Let's call them Bill and Susan. Bill is an IT manager, Susan works in recruitment or something like that. Actually, this is too much detail. Although, while I'm thinking about it, they also have a dog called Buster. Let us say that each of them uses the toilet four times a day. Not the dog, forget the dog. I shouldn't really have mentioned him.

For three of his visits Bill would have the toilet seat up for the purpose of urination (is that the best word? I don't really want to say 'weeing'. Oh, great, now I've said it). For his fourth visit he would have the seat down for the purpose of non-urination (in the chart below I have represented 'Purpose of non-urination' with the letter 'P').

Susan, meanwhile, will have the toilet seat down for all four visits, meaning we don't have to worry about exactly what she's up to.

In the following charts:

S = Susan
B = Bill
B (P) = Bill (purpose of non-urination)

## CHART 1

Let's see what happens when the toilet seat is always left UP.

1. S puts seat down, then back up.
2. B leaves seat alone.
3. S puts seat down, then back up.
4. B leaves seat alone.
5. S puts seat down, then back up.
6. B (P) puts seat down, then back up.
7. S puts seat down, then back up.
8. B leaves seat alone.

In this scenario there are ten interactions with the toilet seat. Susan has eight, and Bill has two.

## CHART 2

Let's see what happens when the toilet seat is always left DOWN.

1. S leaves seat alone.
2. B puts seat up, then back down.
3. S leaves seat alone.
4. B puts seat up, then back down.
5. S leaves seat alone.
6. B (P) leaves seat alone.
7. S leaves seat alone.
8. P puts seat up, then back down.

In this scenario there are only six interactions with the toilet seat, all from Bill. Substantially fewer interactions.

*CHART 3*

Let's see what happens now if everyone just leaves it *exactly where it is* when they've finished.

1.   S puts seat down.
2.   B puts seat up.
3.   S puts seat down.
4.   B puts seat up.
5.   S puts seat down.
6.   B leaves seat alone.
7.   S leaves seat alone.
8.   B puts seat up.

Here we have six interactions again, but this time three for Susan and three for Bill. Which seems fairer.

So, we seemingly have our answer. The fairest way of dealing with the argument is to do *absolutely nothing*. Fantastic news, eh?

However, there is one, even better, solution, but lots of men are not going to like it. The solution is the 'sit-down wee'.

If men truly embraced the sit-down wee it would bring them untold benefits. A wee becomes a time of reflection, a time to read a TV quiz Christmas book, a chance to avoid any form of splashing, and the opportunity to have a very quiet wee, should that be required.

If men decided to sit down every time they went for a wee, the chart would look like this.

*CHART 4*

1. S leaves seat alone.
2. B leaves seat alone.
3. S leaves seat alone.
4. B leaves seat alone.
5. S leaves seat alone.
6. B leaves seat alone.
7. S leaves seat alone.
8. B leaves seat alone.

Result: no toilet-seat interactions AT ALL, no splash anywhere near the loo, and a new air of calm, Zen-like harmony for Bill.

With that solved, just a quick side note. There are some people who believe you should also put the loo lid down. This seems a step too far for me. As if you're pretending that you don't really *have* a toilet. Like those people who hide their TVs in cupboards. Or people who conceal their fridges behind a fake kitchen panel. 'What – *us*? A *fridge*? Hardly.'

# CAN YOU GO ON WEARING CONVERSE FOREVER?

Few things shout 'I'm comfortable in my own skin!' like a pair of Converse All-Stars. Which is ironic because in a pair of Converse All-Stars the one thing in which you cannot guarantee your complete comfort is actually 'your shoes'. For all their pleasing primary-coloured canvas-ness, Converse provide remarkably little by way of podiatric furnishing:* no arch support, nebulous protection against toe-stubbings, or rogue drawing-pins, and precious little by way of grip on the soles. In fact, if you're considering setting foot outside at all you might want to look at a ballet pump or a pair of hiking socks for more all-round durability and practical comfort. But who are we kidding? The attraction of the Converse shoe lies in this very impracticality. This is the shoe of the teenager – moreover, the shoe of the teenager who makes a virtue of

...........................................................................

* Not to be confused with 'paediatric furnishing', which includes high-chairs, bean-bags and Daddy's aching shoulders.

not having thought things through.** Converse are the original Wovver Boots. It's why we love them. We like that our shoes are saying, 'This guy, he don't care,'*** and the older we get, the more we like to cling to this as a statement about ourselves – with each passing year, caring more deeply about not seeming to care.

Until when, though? What is the age after which it's no longer quite right to be so damn carefree? Is there such an age? Think, if it helps, when the cut-off point should be for dating a Kardashian or owning a Ferrari, because the answer is actually the same for all three: you can go on dating Kardashians, driving Ferraris and wearing Converse for as long you can comfortably get in and out of them without asking for help.

.......................................................................................

** Goddammit, they're sometimes so crazy they don't even do up the laces!
*** That's the kind of loose attitude to syntax we want from our casual footwear.

# WHAT'S THE BEST
# THING IN THE WORLD?

The best thing in the whole world? Surely that's an impossible argument to solve. Yep, and that's why it's perfect for this book. We eat impossible for breakfast. With a side order of improbable. All washed down with a lovely cup of massively unlikely. Maybe with some yoghurt.

Finding out the best thing in the entire world comes down to a simple process of elimination. Like so.

*STRICTLY COME DANCING* OR *THE X FACTOR*?
*Strictly Come Dancing*

THE BEATLES OR THE STONES?
The Beatles

CRISTIANO RONALDO OR LIONEL MESSI
Lionel Messi

THE NORTH OR THE SOUTH?

Haha! I'm going nowhere near that one

CHINESE TAKEAWAY, OR INDIAN TAKEAWAY?
Weekdays Chinese, weekend Indian

ADELE OR RIHANNA?
Adele

LOVE OR MONEY?
Love (you *have* to say that, don't you?)

STAYING IN OR GOING OUT?
Staying in: *The Great British Bake Off* is on

SCREAMING AT YOUR EMPLOYEES OR BEING A
DECENT HUMAN BEING?
Being a decent human being

And now, having settled *those* debates, the process continues.
Let's work out what's the best of all of our winners.

QUARTER FINALS
(to be played at Villa Park, Goodison, Hampden and the
Millennium Stadium)

*STRICTLY COME DANCING* V. CHINESE TAKEAWAY
*Strictly Come Dancing*

THE BEATLES V. LIONEL MESSI
The Beatles (this was a close one: injury-time winner from
George Harrison)

ADELE V. BEING A DECENT HUMAN BEING
Being a decent human being

LOVE V. STAYING IN
Love

Which brings us to the semi-finals.

*STRICTLY COME DANCING* V. LOVE
Love

BEING A DECENT HUMAN BEING V. THE BEATLES
Being a decent human being

So what is the very best thing in the entire world? It all comes down to . . .

**LOVE V. BEING A DECENT HUMAN BEING**

And I declare that one a draw.

# DO WE HAVE TO GO TO THIS WEDDING?

I will assume that you would only ever ask this question if the answer wasn't a clear and resounding 'Yes, because we want to.' But for all other considerations here is a foolproof guide.

1.  Is the wedding today? If 'yes', go to 2; if 'no', go to 3.
2.  Have you replied saying, 'Yes we'd love to come'? If 'yes', go to 18; if 'no', go to 7.
3.  Are they close family? If 'yes', go to 17; if 'no', go to 4.
4.  Do you know them through work? If 'yes', go to 5; if 'no', go to 14.
5.  Are you senior or junior to them? If 'senior', go to 6; if 'junior', go to 12.
6.  Are they a valued member of the team, or is this just a desperate bid for promotion? If 'valued', go to 10; if 'promotion', go to 13.
7.  Have you replied? If 'no', go to 8.
8.  You *really* didn't bother replying to someone's wedding

invitation? If 'no', go to 9.

9. Well, you could plead ignorance and say it never arrived. Go to 16.

10. Do you like them? Will there be other people there whom you like? If 'yes' to both, go to 21; if 'no' to either, go to 11.

11. Will you feel guilty if you don't go? If 'yes', go to 21; if 'no', go to 16.

12. You got asked by someone senior to go to their wedding? Get you! Go to 10 above.

13. Is it likely to be quite a flashy wedding? Beyoncé/Cristal/ goodie bags? If 'yes', go to 21; if 'no', go to 10 above.

14. I'm guessing they're friends but not close friends. Do you anticipate still being friends with them in five years' time? If 'yes', go to 10 above; if 'no', go to 15.

15. To be honest, they probably only asked you because someone else pulled out. This was probably the last time you'd see them in either of your lives. Go to 16.

16. Buy them something inexpensive from their list, then go to 19.

17. Do you receive regular Christmas cards from them (or their parents)? If 'yes', go to 21; if 'no', go to 19.

18. Is one of you ill, about to give birth, or at the bedside of a dying friend? If 'yes', go to 19; if 'no', go to 20.

19. NO, YOU DON'T HAVE TO GO.

20. YES, OF COURSE YOU DO. YOU'D BETTER GET GOING. THERE'S ROADWORKS ON THE A414.

21. YES, YOU DO HAVE TO GO.

# DOES GOD EXIST?

Where better to end our book than with the ultimate question? I was tempted to put it at number forty-two as a tribute to Douglas Adams, but I think that this is where it truly belongs.

This question has long been addressed by the greatest philosophers of the age. But, as far as I know, it hasn't been addressed by the sidekick on a daytime quiz show. Until now.

I recognise that it may be a controversial subject, but I'm not scared of controversy. For example, my opinion on 'Who is the best member of One Direction?' was *so* controversial it had to be cut from this book altogether.

Some people, like the Pope and the Archbishop of Canterbury (reminder to self: check this), believe that the universe was created by God, and that he or she continues to exert some influence upon it. Other people, like Professor Brian Cox and Professor Keanu Reeves (again, check), believe we are an extraordinary cosmic accident.

From my own personal perspective, I believe I'm made of the same building blocks as every drop of water, every blade of grass and every speck of dust in the universe, and it is only by an incredibly unlikely and long drawn-out sequence of events that I've gained consciousness. Which is the only reason that I can ask 'Does God exist?' while a blade of grass can't (probably best to check this too).

As for my 'soul' or 'spirit', it didn't exist before I was born so I can't see an argument for why it would exist after I die.

That, for *me*, is a spectacular story with plenty of room for joy and magic, but not for a Creator. I find it utterly mind-blowing, in a good way.

But there is clearly a God-shaped hole in the universe for many people, which is why every society there has ever been has invented their own version of God. To fill the gaps, to answer the questions, to calm the fears. Like flying on an aeroplane, it's nice to think that *someone* is in charge. And it's also nice to have a good book.

As the job of *The 100 Most Pointless Arguments in the World* is to solve all disputes once and for all, I'm going to have to give a definitive yes or no. And if this book becomes the most important document of its age (which I suspect it will, given our conclusions on salt and vinegar crisps and how many cows you can fit into a bedroom) then I have quite a responsibility. I could be about to end all wars or, alternatively, start a whole batch of brand-new ones.

So, this is the way I see it. We only argue about the existence of God because *we care*. Because *all of us* – believers and non-believers – want the world to be a happier, more equal and peaceful place. So which answer causes the least harm here?

If I decide God doesn't exist (and this is *binding*, remember), I remove an immense source of happiness and comfort from the world. And those things are *definitely* real. If I decide that God *does* exist, then all that will happen is a couple of atheists will shrug and go back to wondering exactly what capital city 'What's Missing From Santa's Rindr?' could possibly refer to (see page 274). They might also tut, but I can handle that.

There is no doubt that some people do terrible things in the name of religion. But in any group of people some will be awful. Some people in my office are awful (mentioning no names, Barry from Accounts). And some people do terrible things in the name of, say, football, but I'm still prepared to accept that Rio Ferdinand exists.

So, for the sake of humanity itself, here is the final conclusion:

God *does* exist.*

---

**POINTLESS FACTS**

God is the only character on *The Simpsons* to have a full hand of digits – even Jesus, when he's been on, has only four.

The word 'God' appears in every book of the Bible, except Esther and Song of Solomon.

---

* And Zayn is my favourite member of One Direction. Merry Christmas, one and all!

# ANSWERS

## 95 DO I HAVE THE WORST CATCHPHRASE IN THE WORLD?

1. *Play Your Cards Right* 28
2. *Blockbusters* 54
3. *The Price Is Right* 46
4. *Telly Addicts* 3
5. *Bullseye* 36
6. *Ask the Family* 13
7. *Family Fortunes* 58
8. *Through the Keyhole* 37
9. *University Challenge* 44
10. *Fifteen to One* 6
11. *Busman's Holiday* 1
12. *Who Wants To Be a Millionaire?* 68
13. *Shooting Stars* 17

# 89 ARE WE GOING TO LET RICHARD'S GEEKY WORDPLAY QUIZZES RUIN OUR CHRISTMAS AGAIN?

1. Newport
2. Sheffield (Chef Healed)
3. Liverpool
4. Preston (Pressed On)
5. Cambridge (if the Archers are from Ambridge, then the Carchers are from . . .)
6. Plymouth (Anagram)
7. Ripon
8. Aberdeen (James Dean in Abba)
9. Well, my answer was Ely (Denis 'Ealey) but lots and lots of you put Londonderry, which, given that Derry Irvine was Lord Chancellor, is also a totally valid answer, so both answers are correct! Yay!
10. Leeds
11. Canterbury
12. York (turkeY OR Kenya)
13. Chester (Chest E.R.)
14. Exeter
15. Lisburn
16. Sunderland (S under land)
17. Salford (Anagram)
18. Newcastle ('cleats' an anagram of, and thus 'new' Castle)
19. Dundee

20. Cardiff (funny person = CARD I = I follow on Twitter! = FF). Anyone putting 'Carlisle' for this question, much as I love Clarke Carlisle he's more of a 'footballer I follow on Twitter', and also wouldn't require an exclamation mark at the end of the clue.

21. Newry (newer E)

22. Truro (True Roe)

23. Peterborough (Peter Pan, Peter Cook, Peter Rabbit)

24. Edinburgh (Anagram)

25. Armagh (well, it made me laugh)

26. Hereford (Here Ford. Thanks to @matosman)

27. Portsmouth (Left Port Opening Mouth around 1 September, S)

28. Bristol ('A Left Tit' Would Have Been An Equally Valid Clue)

29. Leicester or Wells

30. Derby (the Derby was famously won many times by Lester Piggott, and, it turns out, less famously in the nineteenth century by John Wells. As I'm accepting Wells, it will now not be used in today's quiz. The clue was going to be 'Fine, Fit and Healthy')

31. St Asaph (Anagram Of Pasta in SH)

32. Gloucester (Boom Boom!)

33. Carlisle (Carl Lewis, Isle of Lewis)

34. Stirling (fish Ling, stir Porridge)

35. Birmingham (Anagram)

36. St Albans (Bans after anagram of Last)

37. Coventry (Coven Try)

38. Inverness (Ern as In 'verness')
39. Hull (Rod Hull)
40. Bath (the answer was hidden in the introduction to the quiz, in the phrase 'joB AT Hand')

## 84 DOES ALL MUSIC SOUND THE SAME THESE DAYS?

1. 'Don't You Worry Child', Swedish House Mafia
2. 'Need U (100%)', Duke Dumont, featuring A*M*E*
3. 'Mama Do The Hump', Rizzle Kicks
4. 'Whistle', Flo Rida
5. 'Turn Around', Conor Maynard
6. 'Can You Hear Me (Ayayaya)', Wiley featuring Skepta, JME & Ms D
7. 'Thrift Shop', Macklemore & Ryan Lewis, featuring Wanz
8. 'Bom Bom', Sam & The Womp
9. 'Scream', Usher
10. 'International Love', Pitbull, featuring Chris Brown
11. 'Ho Hey', The Lumineers
12. 'Sweet Nothing', Calvin Harris, featuring Florence Welch
13. '212', Azealia Banks, featuring Lazy Jay
14. 'Call My Name', Cheryl
15. 'Hey Porsche', Nelly
16. 'Attracting Flies', AlunaGeorge
17. 'Ride Wit Me', Nelly, featuring St Lunatics
18. 'Hall Of Fame', The Script, featuring Will.I.Am

19. 'Latch', Disclosure, featuring Sam Smith
20. 'Not Giving In', Rudimental, featuring John Newman &
    Alex Clare

## 79 SHOULD I WRITE A NOVEL?

1.  *Twilight*, Stephenie Meyer 7
2.  *The Lion, the Witch and the Wardrobe*, C. S. Lewis 41
3.  *Moby-Dick*, Herman Melville 18
4.  *Trainspotting*, Irvine Welsh 15
5.  *Harry Potter and the Philosopher's Stone*, J. K. Rowling 33
6.  *The Good Soldier*, Ford Madox Ford 1
7.  *One Day*, David Nicholls 1
8.  *Nineteen Eighty-Four*, George Orwell 8
9.  *A Tale of Two Cities*, Charles Dickens 16
10. *The War of the Worlds*, H. G. Wells 22
11. *Fifty Shades of Grey*, E. L. James 4 (Finally Uncle Keith
    wins a round)
12. *Bridget Jones's Diary*, Helen Fielding 31

## 75 ARE BANK HOLIDAYS A GOOD IDEA?

1.  Japan  30
2.  India  91
3.  Czech Republic  7
4.  South Africa  3
5.  France  92
6.  Thailand  10

7. USA  97
8. Netherlands  16
9. Spain  48
10. Germany  1
11. Peru  21
12. New Zealand  26


## 72 ENGLISH FOOTBALL MASCOTS –
## BLESSING OR CURSE?

1. Stoke City
2. Sheffield Wednesday
3. Newcastle United
4. Preston North End
5. Fulham
6. Tottenham Hotspur
7. Arsenal
8. Barnet
9. Chelsea
10. Manchester United
11. Brighton & Hove Albion
12. Portsmouth


## 69 IS BEING A BASSIST A PROPER JOB?

1. The Police  53
2. Queen  12
3. Coldplay  4

4. Kiss  28
5. McFly  13
6. U2  18
7. Green Day  3 (So *that*'s who Mike Dirnt is)
8. Rush  6
9. The Beatles  80
10. Led Zeppelin  9
11. Pink Floyd  22
12. The Who  25
13. Muse  1
14. Red Hot Chili Peppers  12


## 64 WHICH IS THE BEST BREED OF CATTLE?

1. Droughtmaster
2. Highland
3. Dexter
4. Belgian Blue
5. Hereford


## 59 WHAT SHOULD I CHANGE MY NAME TO?

1. Lemony Snicket  16
2. George Orwell  52
3. Anthony Burgess  11
4. Joseph Conrad  7
5. James Herriot  34
6. Hergé  1

7. Ruth Rendell  2
8. John Le Carré  10
9. Mark Twain  30
10. Dr Seuss  44
11. Richard Bachman  7
12. Voltaire  5
13. Mary Westmacott 8
14. Lewis Carroll  32

## 56 WHAT IS THE BEST LENGTH FOR A POP SONG?

1.  T. Rex
2.  Duane Eddy & the Rebels
3.  Green Day
4.  Elvis Presley
5.  The Byrds
6.  The Smiths
7.  Blur
8.  The Rolling Stones
9.  The White Stripes
10. The Clash
11. The Beach Boys
12. The Beatles
13. Maurice Williams & the Zodiacs
14. Jonny Trunk & Wisbey

## 51 *IS* THE ONLY WAY IS ESSEX *THE END OF CIVILISATION AS WE KNOW IT?*

1. Jack Straw  3
2. Dermot O'Leary  16
3. Noel Edmonds  52
4. Maggie Smith  14
5. Ian Holm  0!
6. Sally Gunnell  7
7. Denise Van Outen  25
8. Jilly Cooper  14
9. Russell Brand  36
10. Sarah Kane  0!
11. Joan Sims  2
12. Dudley Moore  28

## 47 *DO I HAVE TO CALL LORD SUGAR 'LORD SUGAR'?*

1. Czech Republic  1
2. Spain  16
3. Denmark (I Know, Right?)  6
4. Netherlands  34
5. Egypt  53
6. USA  28
7. France  44
8. Japan  45
9. Mexico  21

10. Germany 1
11. Sweden 2
12. India 12


## 44 ARE FILM REMAKES EVER ANY GOOD?

1. *Footloose*
2. *Sabrina*
3. *King Kong*
4. *Ocean's Eleven*
5. *Total Recall*
6. *The Girl With the Dragon Tattoo*
7. *Alfie*
8. *The Thomas Crown Affair*
9. *The Stepford Wives*
10. *Arthur*
11. *Psycho*
12. *True Grit*


## 38 HOW DO WE FEEL ABOUT POSTMAN PAT?

1. Lawyer
2. Gamekeeper
3. Detective
4. Weaver
5. Chocolatière
6. Teacher
7. Sailor

8. Librarian
9. Doctor
10. Spy
11. Maid
12. Barber

## 34 ARE MENSA MEMBERS DEAD BRAINY?

1. Lucy Irvine
2. Norman Schwarzkopf
3. Goldie Hawn
4. Carol Vorderman
5. Isaac Asimov
6. Steve Martin
7. Dolph Lundgren
8. Geena Davis
9. Quentin Tarantino
10. Clive Sinclair
11. Jamie Theakston
12. Adrian Moorhouse

## 29 ARE BRITISH SPORTS BETTER THAN AMERICAN SPORTS?

1. San Francisco 17
2. Houston 6
3. Chicago 36
4. Philadelphia 40

5. Seattle  14
6. St Louis  3
7. Washington  16
8. Oakland  1
9. Miami  38
10. Cleveland  13
11. Kansas City  5
12. Pittsburgh  23

## 25 WHAT ARE THE BEST AND WORST COVER VERSIONS OF ALL TIME?

1. 'Tainted Love'  32
2. 'Sweet Child O' Mine'  5
3. 'It's Raining Men'  49
4. 'I'll Stand By You'  8
5. 'These Boots Are Made For Walking'  18
6. 'I Just Don't Know What To Do With Myself'  3
7. 'Unchained Melody'  30
8. 'Wonderwall'  22
9. 'I Who Have Nothing'  1
10. 'Tragedy'  31
11. 'Feeling Good'  4
12. 'Axel F'  10
13. 'Without You'  17
14. 'American Pie'  40

## 22 WHICH IS THE BEST CURRENCY IN THE WORLD?

1. Baht
2. Rupee
3. Euro
4. Kuna
5. Forint
6. Zloty
7. Peso
8. Shilling
9. Franc
10. Dinar
11. Won
12. Dollar

## 17 ARE WE GOING TO LET RICHARD'S GEEKY WORDPLAY QUIZZES RUIN OUR CHRISTMAS AGAIN? (PART 2)

1. Santiago (anagram of 'I go Santa')
2. Brasilia (more like a Brazil)
3. Lisbon (Liz -bon)
4. Singapore (singer-poor)
5. Tripoli (triple E)
6. Caracas (crackers, of course)
7. Bucharest (book a rest)
8. Astana (a Stannah)

9. Montevideo ('Monty' video)
10. Seoul (soul)
11. Valetta (a valeter. That's a real job, right?)
12. Baghdad (a bag for Dad. You didn't think I'd forget my dad, surely)
13. Stockholm (home for stock) or Basseterre (baster)
14. Belmopan (anagram of 'lamb'? Nope. Islamabad totally not an acceptable answer for seven or eight reasons, I'm afraid)
15. New Delhi (a new deli. Terrible joke but, hey, it's Christmas!)
16. Bern/Berne (burn)
17. Bangkok (ban cock. Got that out of the way without a rude clue)
18. Beijing (the act of making beige)
19. Paris ('Pa' R I S)
20. Bogotá (chrimBO GOT A)
21. Kingston (King's ton)
22. Ankara (if I anchor ships, what am I)
23. Georgetown (Boy GEORGE town)
24. Dublin (my favourite clue)
25. Amman (pronounced A MAN)
26. Male (written 'male')
27. Castries (anagram)
28. Prague (proper cryptic clue: back-up = PU wrapping around paper RAG, with the 'nog' or head of 'egg', E) My brother Mat wrote this one.

29. Malabo (so dis MAL A BOxing)
30. Budapest (booed a pest)


## 12 FICTIONAL ADDRESSES – DO WE CARE WHERE OUR CHARACTERS LIVE?

1. Gromit
2. Spongebob Squarepants
3. Harry Potter
4. Hilda Ogden
5. Jane Marple
6. Leopold Bloom
7. Frasier Crane
8. Homer Simpson
9. Fitzwilliam Darcy
10. Paddington Bear
11. Sherlock Holmes
12. Buffy Summers


## 7 IS IT EVER OKAY TO WALK OUT BEFORE THE END OF A FILM?

1. *Back to the Future*  13
2. *Sunset Boulevard*  5
3. *The Wizard of Oz*  34
4. *To Kill a Mockingbird*  2
5. *Home Alone*  8
6. *Psycho*  1